Camp Genesis:
Exploring God's Creation

Written by Vanessa Small

Small Publishing | Belleview, Florida

For the campers at West 8th Street.
- V.S.

© **2019 Vanessa Small**
All rights reserved.

ISBN: 978-1-946257-02-4

Permission is granted for the original purchaser to view, download, print, and copy pages for single local church use only. Content may not otherwise be shared, distributed, copied, or sold without express permission from the publisher.

Unless otherwise indicated, Scripture quotations are taken from THE HOLY BIBLE, NEW INTERNATIONAL VERSION®, NIV® Copyright © 1973, 1978, 1984, 2011 by Biblica, Inc.® Used by permission. All rights reserved worldwide.

Scripture quotations marked KJV are taken from the King James Version.

Each page of this curriculum features a unique background picture, displaying the beauty and variety of God's Creation. The photographs were taken by Cheryl Small, Deborah Small, Vincent Small, and Vanessa Small. Photographs © 2019 by Small Publishing.

Small Publishing
P.O. Box 800
Belleview, FL 34421
smallpublishing1@gmail.com

smallpublishing.wordpress.com
facebook.com/SmallPublishing
pinterest.com/SmallPublishing
instagram.com/SmallPublishing

Table of Contents

Director's Guide..1

    Goals and Objectives..3

    Daily Activities Overview Chart.................................4

    Sample Schedule..5

    Guide to the Curriculum..7

    Printable Resources..9

    Volunteers..11

    Registration and Arrival...14

    Communicating with Families.................................16

    Follow-Up..17

Campfire Bible Stories: Bible Lesson Leader's Guide........19

Adventure Trail: Game Leader's Guide..............................43

The Canteen: Snack Leader's Guide...................................67

Creation Crafts: Craft Leader's Guide................................85

Opening and Closing: Daily Leader's Guide....................101

Daily Bible Memory Verses..131

Discover More on Social Media...144

About Camp Genesis...145

Notes:

Camp Genesis:

Exploring God's Creation

Director's Guide

Small Publishing | Belleview, Florida

To the Director:

In Mark 10:14, Jesus said, "Let the little children come to me, and do not hinder them, for the kingdom of God belongs to such as these."

As the director of Camp Genesis, you're living out that very command. You have the great privilege and responsibility of helping children discover the truth of who God is and what He has done and of leading them to a faith-filled relationship with Him.

Please take a moment in prayer and ask God to prepare your heart as you seek to serve Him and His children. Remember, your job is to be a model of God's love.

When you're ready, turn the page and get ready to lead kids on an exciting adventure in God's Word as we discover His amazing Creation and get to know our great Creator!

*"The heavens declare the glory of God;
the skies proclaim the work of his hands."*
(Psalm 19:1)

In the beginning God ...

There are many theories in our world today about where we came from and how our universe originated. "**By faith we understand that the universe was formed at God's command, so that what is seen was not made out of what was visible**" (Hebrews 11:3). Throughout history, God has revealed Himself through His Word and His Creation. **Camp Genesis leads children on an exciting exploration of both God's Word and His Creation, building a foundation of faith in their lives as they get to know their Creator better.** Children will discover God's care for all of His Creation – each family, each child. Our hope is that as children take a closer look at God's created world, their response will be to praise the Creator who designed it all and put their trust in Him. "**You are worthy, our Lord and God, to receive glory and honor and power, for you created all things, and by your will they were created and have their being**" (Revelation 4:11).

Goals and Objectives

Success is often determined by attendance numbers, but there are other measures of success to consider as you plan and implement your program. Some of the goals and objectives of the Camp Genesis program include:

- To reach children from the community and connect with families, helping children to build positive relationships with other children and also adults from the church.
- To help children feel comfortable in the church environment and realize that learning about God can be fun.
- To help children learn about the Bible and understand a specific set of truths from God's Word including the fact that God created the world and cares for His Creation.
- To convey to children and families the fact that Jesus loves them and so do we!
- To encourage children to respond in praise to their Creator and begin (or continue to grow in) a relationship with Him.

Camp Genesis was originally written as a five-day Vacation Bible School program. However, it can also be used in other settings including day camps or other special summer events. You can also use one lesson each week for a five-week study for your weekend services or mid-week programs.

Camp Genesis
Daily Activities Overview

Day 1	Day 2	Day 3	Day 4	Day 5
God created the heavens and the earth.	God cares for His Creation.	I will praise God, my Creator.	God makes me grow.	God made my family.
Bible Memory Verse: Genesis 1:1	**Bible Memory Verse:** 1 Peter 5:7	**Bible Memory Verse:** Psalm 150:6	**Bible Memory Verse:** Galatians 5:22-23	**Bible Memory Verse:** Joshua 24:15
Campfire Bible Stories: In the Beginning	**Campfire Bible Stories:** Big or Small, God Cares for All	**Campfire Bible Stories:** Let All Creation Praise the Lord	**Campfire Bible Stories:** Growing Like Jesus	**Campfire Bible Stories:** The First Family
Adventure Trail Games: Days of Creation Relay	**Adventure Trail Games:** Creation Scavenger Hunt	**Adventure Trail Games:** Pavement Praise	**Adventure Trail Games:** Good Fruit/ Bad Fruit	**Adventure Trail Games:** Family Night Carnival
The Canteen Snacks: Creation Cups	**The Canteen Snacks:** Edible Bird Nests	**The Canteen Snacks:** Praise Him S'more	**The Canteen Snacks:** Seed-bearing Fruit	**The Canteen Snacks:** Family Faces
Creation Crafts: Creation Collages	**Creation Crafts:** Recycled Birdfeeders	**Creation Crafts:** Praise Rocks	**Creation Crafts:** Plant People	**Creation Crafts:** Stick Figure Families

Sample Schedule

The Camp Genesis program has been designed to include four 20-minute stations, as well as a 20-minute opening time and a 20-minute closing time each day. A sample schedule is provided below, allowing for five-minute breaks in between each station to give groups time to move from one place to the next. Going by this schedule would result in a 2 ½-hour per day program. However, this time can be lengthened or shortened depending on your ministry's needs. For example, singing a greater or fewer number of songs during the opening and closing would alter the total amount of time. Also, station leaders can adapt their material as needed to allow for longer or shorter rotation times.

Sample Schedule for Days 1–4

6:05 – 6:25 p.m. – Opening

6:30 – 6:50 p.m. – Station 1

6:55 – 7:15 p.m. – Station 2

7:20 – 7:40 p.m. – Station 3

7:45 – 8:05 p.m. – Station 4

8:10 – 8:30 p.m. – Closing

Sample Schedule for Day 5

6:05 – 6:25 p.m. – Opening

6:30 – 6:50 p.m. – Station 1

6:55 – 7:15 p.m. – Station 2

7:20 – 7:40 p.m. – Closing Ceremony

7:45 – 8:30 p.m. – Family Night Carnival

Days 1-4 Rotation Schedule

	GROUP 1	GROUP 2	GROUP 3	GROUP 4
OPENING	Opening	Opening	Opening	Opening
STATION 1	Creation Crafts	The Canteen Snacks	Campfire Bible Stories	Adventure Trail Games
STATION 2	Adventure Trail Games	Campfire Bible Stories	Creation Crafts	The Canteen Snacks
STATION 3	The Canteen Snacks	Creation Crafts	Adventure Trail Games	Campfire Bible Stories
STATION 4	Campfire Bible Stories	Adventure Trail Games	The Canteen Snacks	Creation Crafts
CLOSING	Closing	Closing	Closing	Closing

Day 5 Rotation Schedule

Families are invited to join their children for the last half of the day's programming.

	GROUP 1	GROUP 2	GROUP 3	GROUP 4
OPENING	Opening	Opening	Opening	Opening
STATION 1	Campfire Bible Stories	Campfire Bible Stories	Creation Crafts	Creation Crafts
STATION 2	Creation Crafts	Creation Crafts	Campfire Bible Stories	Campfire Bible Stories
CLOSING	Closing Ceremony			
CARNIVAL	Family Night Carnival (including Games and Snacks)			

Guide to the Curriculum

This is your road map to the Camp Genesis curriculum. Below is a list of all resources included in this curriculum. Under each section name, you will find a description of the resource along with instructions on how to use it. Visit our blog at http://smallpublishing.wordpress.com for additional resources. Resources with Scripture quotations are provided in both the NIV and KJV so you can choose which version you would like to use. Permission is granted for the original purchaser of this curriculum to view, download, print, and copy pages for single local church use only. Content may not otherwise be shared, distributed, copied, or sold without express permission from the publisher.

Campfire Bible Stories – Leader's Guide

- Copy and give this section of curriculum to the Bible lesson station leader.
- You should also read through the Bible lesson leader's guide so you as a director will know what will be taking place in this station and so you will know what the leader will need and how you can assist him or her. A supply list is included in the guide.
- Encourage the leader of this station to provide time for the children to share their thoughts and questions. While it is important to stick to the leader's guide, it is also important to discuss the concepts with the children and get feedback from them to see if they are understanding. Review as necessary.
- Printable resources referred to in the curriculum are available for download on our blog at http://smallpublishing.wordpress.com.

Adventure Trail Games – Leader's Guide

- Copy and give this section of curriculum to the game station leader.
- You should also read through the game leader's guide so you as a director will know what will be taking place in this station and so you will know what the leader will need and how you can assist him or her. A supply list is included in the guide.
- Each day's activities can take place either outdoors or indoors. If you choose to hold them outdoors, have an alternate indoor location reserved in case of inclement weather. The game leader's guide provides instructions for adapting each activity to an indoor setting if needed.
- This guide gives instructions for a closing family night carnival to be held on Day 5 of Camp Genesis. Coordinate with the game leader as you plan for this event. See the Rotation Schedule for an alternate schedule for Day 5 to allow time for the carnival. Invite families to join their children during this special closing event.
- Printable resources referred to in the curriculum are available for download on our blog at http://smallpublishing.wordpress.com.

The Canteen Snacks – Leader's Guide

- Copy and give this section of curriculum to the snack station leader.
- You should also read through the snack leader's guide so you as a director will know what will be taking place in this station and so you will know what the leader will need and how you can assist him or her. A supply list is included in the guide.
- Be sure the snack leader is informed of any food allergies listed on the children's registration forms.
- Ask someone who is not assigned to a particular group or station to take a head count of each group (children and volunteers) during the daily opening and report those numbers to the snack leaders so they can prepare an adequate number of snacks.
- You may want to have sandwiches, such as peanut butter and jelly, available each day in addition to that day's regular snack. Some children may come without having eaten lunch or supper, and they will learn better if their needs are satisfied.

Creation Crafts – Leader's Guide

- Copy and give this section of curriculum to the craft station leader.
- You should also read through the craft leader's guide so you as a director will know what will be taking place in this station and so you will know what the leader will need and how you can assist him or her. A supply list is included in the guide.
- Printable resources referred to in the curriculum are available for download on our blog at http://smallpublishing.wordpress.com.

Opening and Closing – Leader's Guide

- Copy and give this section of curriculum to the opening and closing leader.
- You should also read through the opening and closing leader's guide so you as a director will know what will be taking place in this station and so you will know what the leader will need and how you can assist him or her.
- Choose a missions project to support. Try to choose something that can be explained concretely to children so they will understand how their offering is making a difference. Throughout the program, encourage the children to participate by bringing in coins or food items to give to a local food bank, charity, or missionary. Let families know that this voluntary offering will be collected each day during Camp Genesis.
- Music is not included with this curriculum; however, please visit the Small Publishing page on Pinterest for suggested songs that correspond with the Camp Genesis theme.

Daily Bible Memory Verses

- A new Bible memory verse will be introduced each day in the opening. Encourage leaders to review these verses with the children throughout each day of camp.
- Hang up a set of Bible memory verse posters at each station. Color versions of these posters are available on our blog at http://smallpublishing.wordpress.com.

Printable Resources

The following resources are available on our blog at http://smallpublishing.wordpress.com.

Printable Certificate

- Give a copy of this certificate to each child who attends your Camp Genesis program, even those who were not in attendance for all five days. Write the child's name on the line, and have your pastor or ministry leader sign and date the certificate. The certificates can be presented to the children during the closing on Day 5 of your Camp Genesis program or during any special closing activities you may plan for your weekend services following the conclusion of Camp Genesis.

Printable Charts

- This file contains printer-friendly versions of the Daily Activities Overview Chart and the Rotation Schedule. Each volunteer should have a copy of these. These charts are also included in the Director's Guide and the Volunteer's Guide, but you may want to make some extra copies to have on hand in case a leader needs one.

Printable Postcards

- Print this file on the front and back of a piece of card stock (or have it professionally printed). Cut the page in quarters to create four postcard invitations you can mail or give out at your church or other locations in the community to help spread the word.
- Write your church's name and address in the top left corner of the postcard or use a return address label. Add the dates and times of your program as well as contact information such as a phone number or email address for those who want more information.

Printable Posters

- *Station Name Posters*: Print a set of these posters to hang on the door of each station location. You can also make additional sets of the posters to hang up as directional signs. Draw an arrow on the sign, and hang it up on the wall or down a hallway to direct group leaders and children as to where each station is located. Add a construction paper frame to the black-and-white posters to add a splash of color.
- *Daily Bible Memory Verse Posters*: Print a set of the Bible memory verse posters to hang up at each station. The posters are available in the New International Version (NIV) as well as the King James Version (KJV).
- *Promotional Posters*: Print copies of these posters to advertise your camp. In the empty space on each poster, write in the details of your program including dates and times, location, and contact information. Hang them up in your church or ministry facility as well as other locations in your community to get the word out about your event.

Printable Resources for Station Activities

- The following activities have corresponding printable resources that are referred to in the station leader guides:
    - Campfire Bible Stories - Day 5
    - Creation Crafts - Days 1, 4, 5
    - Adventure Trail Games - Day 2
- Download each resource from our blog, print enough copies for each child, and give to the appropriate station leader.

Printable Registration Form

- A sample blank registration form is available on our blog. Make copies of this form for the registration table. You will need one registration form per child.

Printable Volunteer Appreciation Resource

- Be sure to include a time of recognition for all of the volunteers who help with your Camp Genesis program. You can do this during the closing ceremony on Day 5 or during your weekend services following the conclusion of Camp Genesis.
- This resource provides instructions for a simple and inexpensive memento you can present your volunteers. Print copies of the page, and cut out the rectangles. Tape one rectangle to the front of a packet of seeds, and give one seed packet to each volunteer. Remind your volunteers that by serving at Camp Genesis, they have planted spiritual seeds in the lives of the children, and God will be faithful to make those seeds grow and bear fruit (see 1 Corinthians 3:5-9).
- Be sure to also thank those who have helped by donating supplies or praying for the program as well as the parents and families who allowed their children to attend.
- Please visit our blog at http://smallpublishing.wordpress.com for information on the *Ministry Gift Book* series from Small Publishing, another gift option to show your appreciation for all who took part in serving the children at Camp Genesis.

Printable Volunteer's Guide

- All volunteers will need a copy of the Camp Genesis Volunteer's Guide. This will give your volunteers an overview of the program's theme and activities as well as an introduction to the rules and procedures in place for your camp.
- Print copies of the guides, cut the pages in half, and staple the pages to form a booklet.
- Distribute these at a training session to all leaders and helpers, and read or summarize each page for them during this training time. One of the most important parts of this training will be to go over all of the policies, procedures, rules, and expectations with the leaders and helpers. This is essential to maintaining consistency with the children and ensuring their safety. Fill in the blanks provided, and adapt the rules and policies as needed to fit your unique ministry.

Volunteers

It takes a team! Everyone working together and doing his or her part makes Camp Genesis what it is! See below for a detailed list of all volunteer roles. You and some of the volunteers may be able to fill more than one role, but delegate responsibility when possible in order to allow others to experience the joy of serving and to help take the load off your shoulders. Many people are willing to help if you ask them personally, but they may not feel comfortable volunteering on their own. Find out what their gifts are and where they would be successful.

- **Director**
    - That's you! As the director, you are responsible to oversee the Camp Genesis volunteer team. Don't get overwhelmed, but trust God to do His work!
- **Station Leaders and Helpers** (Crafts, Snacks, Games, Bible Lessons)
    - One main leader is needed for each of the four stations, as well as helpers who will assist the station leader. Each leader will be responsible for preparing and presenting his or her daily activity four times each day as each group rotates through the station.
- **Opening and Closing Leader**
    - This leader will be responsible for leading the daily opening and closing gatherings that all groups attend together.
- **Song Leader**
    - If the opening and closing leader is not comfortable leading the music, you will need to recruit a song leader who will lead the children in singing during the opening and closing gatherings.
- **Camp Counselors and Assistants**
    - These volunteers will remain with one group of children throughout the entire program and guide them in rotating from station to station. They are not responsible for teaching or leading any lessons, but they should talk with the children about what they are learning, practice the Bible memory verse with the children throughout the day, and be open to any questions the children might have. You will need at least two volunteers per group of children, but depending on the size of the groups, you will want additional volunteers in each group to maintain an acceptable ratio.
- **Teen Helpers**
    - Teenagers who would like to volunteer at Camp Genesis can be utilized in a variety of areas. They can serve as assistant group leaders to rotate from station to station with one group. They could also serve as assistants in the craft, snack, or game stations. Teenagers may also be recruited to help lead songs and do motions along with the music.

- **Bell Buzzer**
    - Have someone designated to ring a bell or give another type of signal about five minutes before each station rotation time so groups can finish what they are doing. Ring the bell again when it is time to rotate. Inform the station leaders ahead of time what these signals mean.
- **Technology Team**
    - It is good to have volunteers dedicated solely to the technology needs of your camp. During the opening and closing gatherings, this would mean running the sound system, playing music over the speakers at the appropriate time, advancing the slides, etc.
- **Photographers**
    - You will also want to recruit photographers who will take pictures of all the activities that take place and create a slideshow of photos to play during the closing each day.
- **Promotion Coordinator**
    - Designate a person or committee in charge of promoting and advertising your Camp Genesis program. Take advantage of free promotional opportunities in your community such as radio, newspaper, community bulletin boards, and word of mouth. You may also want to send postcards to children, make fliers to distribute around the neighborhood, hang up banners on your property, and include an insert in your church's bulletin and encourage congregation members to give it to a child they know.
- **Supply Organizer**
    - You may want to ask members of your congregation to donate any supplies your church does not already have, or organize a fundraiser to raise money to purchase supplies. A person or committee can be assigned to make sure all supplies have been collected and to purchase any supplies that are not donated. The supply organizer(s) can also help by distributing the appropriate supplies to each station.
- **Registration Specialists**
    - Recruit volunteers to help at the registration table as children arrive each day.
- **Security Team**
    - Have adult volunteers stationed at each entrance during arrival and dismissal times to help ensure that no children leave the building without a parent, guardian, or leader. Depending on the size of your church or ministry facility, you may want to have these individuals remain near the entrances or in the hallways not just during arrival and dismissal times but also while the activities are taking place, especially if your doors are left unlocked during the entire program. The children's safety is of the utmost importance!

- **Nursery Workers**
  - If you have volunteers with children too young to participate in Camp Genesis, you may want to have a staffed nursery available to care for these children.
- **First Aid Worker**
  - Designate a go-to person who is trained in first aid procedures in case minor treatment is needed during your program.
- **Prayer Warriors**
  - Be sure to encourage all of your volunteers as well as your entire church to be praying for the kids, families, and leaders. The congregation's prayer support is crucial!
- **If you have other volunteers who are not able to commit to a major role in your program but still want to be involved in some way, consider these ideas:**
  - Volunteers who cannot attend during the actual program can help ahead of time by setting up and decorating your classrooms and gathering areas. Organize a work day on which volunteers can help complete such tasks.
  - Volunteers can cut out and organize supplies that will be used in the craft station.
  - Volunteers can be present during arrival or dismissal times to serve as greeters and talk to the children.
  - Volunteers who are only able to serve on one day can help by leading a carnival game on the last day of Camp Genesis. This requires a commitment of only a couple of hours.

- **Additional Volunteer Resources:**
  - All volunteers will need a copy of the Camp Genesis Volunteer's Guide. This will give your volunteers an overview of the program's theme and activities as well as an introduction to the rules and procedures in place for your camp. This resource can be found on our blog at http://smallpublishing.wordpress.com.
  - Be sure to continually express your gratitude and appreciation for your Camp Genesis volunteers as they are serving the Lord and His children. A printable Volunteer Appreciation Resource is available to download on our blog, providing instructions for a simple yet meaningful memento you can present to your volunteers at the end of camp.

Registration and Arrival

- **Registration**: Follow your ministry's standard check-in procedures. A sample blank registration form is available on our blog at http://smallpublishing.wordpress.com. Have the children's parents or guardians fill this out to ensure you receive accurate and complete information including allergies and emergency contact information.
- **Nametags**: At the registration table, have children and leaders create nametags for themselves when they arrive. Cut apart individual sticky address labels, and have individuals use markers to write their first names on the labels to stick on their shirts. Having children make a nametag each day helps to create a routine for the children from the moment they walk in the door. The nametags will also help leaders throughout the program, enabling them to call children by name.
- **Assign each child to one of the four groups**. The children will remain with the same group throughout the entire Camp Genesis program and will rotate through the various stations with this group. Assign a color to each group. Add a colored sticker to each child's nametag that corresponds to the color of his or her group.
- Here is one example of how you may choose to divide the groups based on age:
    - **Group 1** – Preschool
    - **Group 2** – Kindergarten and First Grade
    - **Group 3** – Second through Fifth Grade Boys
    - **Group 4** – Second through Fifth Grade Girls
- You may need to rearrange the division of your groups in order to have a more equal number of children in each group. Some children may request to be in the same group as a friend or sibling, so you may choose to accommodate these requests if possible.
- **Early Arrival Activity**: It is important to have an activity the children can immediately begin working on if they arrive early before it is time to begin the opening. This will help to keep them occupied and avoid having them run loose or wander off into areas where they should not be. Once children have registered and made a nametag, direct them to your early arrival activity area. Have adults stationed at all doors to ensure that no children leave the building once they have entered, unless accompanied by a parent or leader.

- In advance, print and cut out small clip art pictures of various things God created. Lay the pictures out on tables, along with supplies the children can use to color. Using roll paper, create a large banner with the words of Genesis 1:1 written on it. Have this banner hanging on the wall before children arrive. As children finish coloring pictures, they can be taped up on the banner, or the pictures can be collected from the children and taped up at a later time. Children are welcome to color several pictures each day, so be sure to have plenty available for them. Throughout Camp Genesis, the banner will become filled with pictures of things God created as the children add more each day. The children can continue working on their pictures until the countdown to the opening begins and it is time to be seated for the opening.
- Designate an area where each group will sit during the opening and closing. For example, assign each group one pew. Tape colored signs to both ends of the pew to correspond to the group's color. You may want to remove items from the seating area, such as hymnals or offering envelopes, so they are not a distraction.

Communicating with Families

Keeping the parents and families informed about what their children are doing and learning throughout the Camp Genesis program is important. You may want to make some notes or fliers to send home with the children during the program to give their families information about upcoming activities.

- Inform the parents that an offering will be taken each day. Describe the specific missions project you have chosen to support. Advise them as to what items the children are welcome to bring (e.g., canned food, coins), but let them know their participation is completely voluntary.

- To help build excitement and unity, each day at Camp Genesis will feature a "color of the day." All children and volunteers are encouraged (but not required) to wear the specified color each day. Inform parents of the "colors of the day" so they can help their children dress accordingly.

Day 1:	Day 2:	Day 3:	Day 4:	Day 5:
Blue	Red	Purple	Green	Orange

- Give parents and families a copy of the day's Bible memory verse when they come to pick their children up each day and encourage them to work on memorizing the verse with their children.

- Let parents know they are welcome to come back 20 minutes early each day if they would like to observe the daily closing time and see a review of what the children have been doing and learning that day. They would also enjoy seeing the daily photo slideshow featuring their children's pictures.

- Invite the children's family members to attend a special final closing ceremony at the conclusion of Camp Genesis. During this time, you can distribute certificates to each child, show photos from the entire program, sing some of the songs the children learned while at camp, give a recap of what was learned and activities that were completed, and thank the families and volunteers. An alternate schedule is suggested for Day 5 of the Camp Genesis program to make this a family night with special closing activities including a carnival. You may also choose to have a separate closing program during your weekend service instead of or in addition to the Day 5 family night activities. Distribute invitations to the family night carnival and also to your church's weekend services. Be sure to include all pertinent information including dates, times, location, etc.

Follow-Up

- After Camp Genesis is over, take a deep breath! You made it! However, there are still some very important follow-up tasks to be completed.
- Post-Camp Contact: Try to make some sort of contact with the children who attended Camp Genesis. Send them a letter telling them you were glad they could join you. Invite them to the next activity or event at your church. Let them know you are praying for them. Include a photograph from their time at camp, and be sure to send photos to the families who gave their contact information at the family photo booth during the closing carnival.
- Keep praying for the children and their families after Camp Genesis. Encourage the prayer warriors of your congregation to continue praying for the children as well. Make a bookmark containing the first names of all the children who attended Camp Genesis. Keep a bookmark in your Bible to remind you to pray for the children, and give bookmarks to others in your church as well. (For safety and privacy, only use first names.)
- Give your pastor or ministry leader a list of attendance figures and contact information for the children and families who attended.

Notes:

Camp Genesis:
Exploring God's Creation

Campfire Bible Stories

Bible Lesson Leader's Guide

Small Publishing | Belleview, Florida

To the Bible Lesson Leader:

In Mark 10:14, Jesus said, "Let the little children come to me, and do not hinder them, for the kingdom of God belongs to such as these."

As a Camp Genesis volunteer, you're living out that very command. You have the great privilege and responsibility of helping children discover the truth of who God is and what He has done and of leading them to a faith-filled relationship with Him.

Please take a moment in prayer and ask God to prepare your heart as you seek to serve Him and His children. Remember, your job is to be a model of God's love.

When you're ready, turn the page and get ready to lead kids on an exciting adventure in God's Word as we discover His amazing Creation and get to know our great Creator!

"The heavens declare the glory of God; the skies proclaim the work of his hands."
(Psalm 19:1)

Campfire Bible Stories

Bible Lessons

Day 1: In the Beginning

Children will take a closer look at the first chapter of Genesis as they discover what God created each day. (Scripture Background: Genesis 1-2)

Day 2: Big or Small, God Cares for All

Children will discover that God cares for all creatures, big or small, and all of our worries, big or small. (Scripture Background: Matthew 6:25-34)

Day 3: Let All Creation Praise the Lord

Children will observe various rocks and discover what it means for us (and the rocks) to praise God. (Scripture Background: Luke 19:28-40)

Day 4: Growing Like Jesus

Children will learn what plants need in order to grow and discover what helps us grow more like Jesus. (Scripture Background: Galatians 5:13-26)

Day 5: The First Family

Children will learn about the very first family and discover God's intent for us to love Him and one another. (Scripture Background: Genesis 2-4)

Supply List
for Campfire Bible Stories

(See the teaching instructions for the individual days for more details about supplies.)

All Days:
- ☐ Camping tent
- ☐ Pretend campfire
- ☐ Carpet squares
- ☐ Bible memory verse posters
- ☐ Bibles

Day 1 – In the Beginning:
- ☐ Bibles
- ☐ Bookmarks or sticky tabs
- ☐ Seven poster boards
- ☐ Pictures of Creation
- ☐ Hook and loop fasteners
- ☐ Seven large envelopes
- ☐ Toy magnifying glasses

Day 2 – Big or Small, God Cares for All:
- ☐ Poster board
- ☐ Bird finger puppet (or small picture of a bird)
- ☐ Bible
- ☐ Paper plates

Day 3 – Let All Creation Praise the Lord:
- ☐ Variety of rocks
- ☐ Palm branches
- ☐ Coats, jackets, or sweaters
- ☐ Paper
- ☐ Music player (e.g., CD or mp3 player)
- ☐ Rhythm instruments
- ☐ Chocolate rocks, popping candy rocks, or rock candy pieces

Day 4 – Growing Like Jesus:
- ☐ Four plants or flowers
- ☐ Green and brown paper
- ☐ Construction paper
- ☐ Tape
- ☐ Bible

Day 5 – The First Family:
- ☐ Construction paper
- ☐ Fruity snacks
- ☐ Printer paper
- ☐ Crayons, markers, or colored pencils

Introduction
for the Bible Lesson Leader

Daily Supplies Needed in the Bible Lesson Station:

- Camping tent
- Pretend campfire
- Carpet squares
- Bible memory verse posters
- Bibles

General Instructions for the Bible Lesson Leader:

- To help make your Campfire Bible Stories station feel more like a "camp," set up a small tent in the room and create a pretend campfire in the middle of your classroom. Place carpet squares for children to sit on in a circle around the campfire. (For more decorating ideas, visit the Small Publishing page on Pinterest.)
- Have posters hanging in your classroom with the daily Bible memory verses printed on them. Review these with the children each day during your lesson time. Repetition will help the children learn these verses.
- If your ministry has enough funds, purchase children's Bibles to give to each child who attends Camp Genesis, especially those who do not already have their own copy of God's Word. Distribute these on the first day of camp. As new campers begin attending, be sure they receive a Bible as well. Encourage the children to bring their Bibles to camp each day, and help them become familiar with how to navigate their Bibles.
- The following lessons are designed to get children actively involved in what they are learning, rather than just passively listening to the teacher. They are also created to appeal to various learning styles.

DAY 1: Bible Lesson
In the Beginning

Supplies Needed:

- Bibles
- Bookmarks or sticky tabs
- Seven poster boards
- Pictures of Creation
- Hook and loop fasteners
- Seven large envelopes
- Toy magnifying glasses

Preparation:

- This lesson is based on Genesis 1-2. Read this passage to help you prepare to teach this lesson.
- Have enough Bibles available for each child to use during this lesson. Place a bookmark or sticky tab in each Bible on the page where the book of Genesis begins. Make sure the bookmarks are in the right spot after each station rotation.
- At the top of one poster, write "Day 1." Continue writing in this way on each poster through Day 7. Hang these posters in order on the wall of your classroom.
- Print small clip art pictures or photographs to represent the things God created each day. If possible, laminate the pictures to help them hold up through all station rotations. For day one, write the words "light," "day," and "night" on bright or dark paper rather than using pictures to represent these abstract concepts. You will not need any pictures for Day 7.

    Day 1: light, day, night   Day 2: sky, clouds
    Day 3: plants, trees, flowers, fruit   Day 4: sun, moon, stars
    Day 5: fish, sea creatures, birds   Day 6: animals, people

- Attach one side of a hook and loop fastener to the back of each picture. Attach the other side of the fastener to the corresponding day's poster.
- Write a number on each envelope starting with 1 and going through 7. Put the pictures corresponding with each day in the appropriate envelopes. Leave envelope 7 empty.

Teaching Instructions:

- Welcome to Camp Genesis where we will be exploring God's Creation! God has created so many good things, but I would like you to close your eyes for a moment and imagine what it would be like if there were no people, no plants, no animals, no sky, no land, no oceans, and no light. *(Pause for a moment and let the children imagine. Then have them open their eyes.)* Before trees, or animals, or the sky, or the sun, or the moon, or the stars, or the oceans, or any people existed – before all of that – there was God. Then, God made all of these things. He created them all.
- The Bible tells us about what happened at the very beginning of the world, when God made these things. We are going to go exploring in our Bibles today to discover more about what God made. *(Distribute a Bible to each child.)*
- The Bible is a very special book that God gave us to help us learn more about Him, how much He loves us, and how He wants us to live. It is different from other books, because it was inspired by God. Every word in the Bible is true.
- The Bible is one big book that is made up of 66 smaller books. The reason our camp is called Camp Genesis is that Genesis is the very first book of the Bible. It is at the very beginning. In fact, that is what the word Genesis means. Genesis means beginning. It is the very first book in God's special book – the Bible.
- That is what we will explore at Camp Genesis – what happened in the very beginning when God first created the world. *(Distribute a magnifying glass to each child.)* Let's open our Bibles and use our magnifying glasses to start exploring God's Word.
- There is a bookmark in your Bible that points to the page where the book of Genesis begins. Turn to that page and see if you can find the title that says "Genesis." It starts with the letter G. Put your finger on it when you find it. *(Allow children time to find the book of Genesis in their Bibles. Help those children who may need assistance.)*
- Under the title of Genesis, you should see a big number one. Put your finger on that number one. *(Give children time to locate the big number one. Observe the students to see that they have all located the correct spot.)* That number one shows us that this is the very first chapter in the book of Genesis. Genesis chapter one tells us about what God created in the beginning.
- As we explore this chapter, I have some mystery envelopes that will help us. I am looking for some good listeners to help open these envelopes. *(Choose two or three volunteers to come to the front as you open each envelope. Let them pull the pictures out of the envelope and attach them to the corresponding numbered poster. Once the volunteers are seated, ask children to raise their hands and name something they see in those pictures. Then summarize for the children what God created on that day by telling the following facts.)*
- Day 1: On the first day, God said, "Let there be light." God spoke, and there was light. God separated the light from the darkness to make day and night. There was evening and there was morning, and that was the very first day.

- Day 2: On the second day, God made the sky. The clouds represent the sky that God created. There was evening, and there was morning. That was the second day.
- Day 3: At this point, water was covering the entire earth. On the third day, God gathered the waters, so that dry ground would appear, so on this day God created the oceans and the land. He also made things grow on the land – trees with fruit and all kinds of plants. There was evening, and there was morning. That was the third day.
- Day 4: On the fourth day, God made two big lights in the sky. God made the greater light, called the sun, to shine in the sky during the day. God also made the moon for the night sky. On this day, God also made all the stars. There was evening, and there was morning. That was the fourth day.
- Day 5: On the fifth day, God made birds and fish. God made all the birds with wings that fly in the sky, and God made all the sea creatures that live in the waters. There was evening, and there was morning. That was the fifth day.
- Day 6: On the sixth day, God made many different kinds of animals. He made livestock animals like the ones that live on farms. He made all the creatures that move along the ground. God also made all the wild animals. God also created something else very special on the sixth day. God made a human being. The very first person that God created was named Adam. Adam was different from all of God's other creations, because humans were created in God's image. There was evening, and there was morning. That was the sixth day.
- (Before moving on to the seventh envelope, briefly review all the things God created on the previous six days.) Everything that God created was very good.
- (Hold out the last envelope to a volunteer and have that person reach in to pull out what is inside, as the children have been doing for the previous days. The children will be surprised to discover there is nothing in this envelope. Ask the group why they think the envelope is empty, and allow them to respond.)
- Day 7: We have nothing to put on our Day 7 poster. It is blank, because the seventh envelope was empty. God created many things on the first six days. By the seventh day, God had finished His work of creating. On the seventh day, God rested from His work. God made the seventh day a very special day. God did not do any creating on that day, but He enjoyed all that He had already created. It was very good.
- Let's pray and tell God thank You for all He has created. (Lead the children in prayer.)
- (If you have extra time, discuss with the children some of their favorite things that God created. For example, what is your favorite fruit God created on the third day? What is your favorite animal God created on the sixth day?)

Special Note for the Leader:

- After each station rotation, remove the pictures from the posters and replace in the envelopes. Tape can be used as an alternative to the hook and loop fasteners if needed.

DAY 2: Bible Lesson

Big or Small, God Cares for All

Supplies Needed:

- Poster board
- Bird finger puppet (or small picture of a bird)
- Bible
- Paper plates

Preparation:

- This lesson is based on Matthew 6:25-34. Read this passage to help you prepare to teach this lesson.
- On a poster board, write "Big or small, God cares for all." Hang this sign up at the front of the classroom.
- On paper plates, draw faces to represent the following expressions: happy, sad, angry, and worried. Draw one face per plate. Make two of each expression.

Teaching Instructions:

- Welcome back, campers! Yesterday, we talked about all of the things God created. Today, we are talking about how God cares for all of His Creation.
- (*Point to the poster, and read it to the children.*) Big or small, God cares for all. Can you say that with me? (*Have the children repeat the phrase along with you.*)
- I am going to name some animals that God created. If I name an animal that is big, I want you to stand up very tall and reach your arms up toward the sky to show that the animal is very big. (*Demonstrate the motions for the children, and have them do the same.*) If I name an animal that is small, I want you to crouch down low to the ground. (*Demonstrate this motion for the children, and have them do it along with you.*) Good job.
- Are you ready? Here we go. The first animal is a lion. Is a lion big or small? (*Allow the children to choose the appropriate motion to show that a lion is big.*) Yes, a lion is big.

- (*Do the same with the following list of animals. Ask the children whether each animal is big or small, and allow them to choose the appropriate motion.*)
    - Ant (*small*)
    - Elephant (*big*)
    - Butterfly (*small*)
    - Whale (*big*)
    - Hamster (*small*)
    - Baby chick (*small*)
    - Bear (*big*)
    - Mouse (*small*)

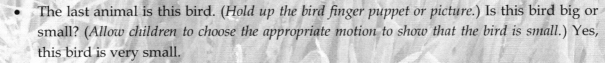

- The last animal is this bird. (*Hold up the bird finger puppet or picture.*) Is this bird big or small? (*Allow children to choose the appropriate motion to show that the bird is small.*) Yes, this bird is very small.
- That was the last animal, so please sit down. (*Allow children to sit down in their spots.*)
- Do you think that because this bird is so small, God forgets about the little bird and does not care about it? (*Allow children to respond.*) No, big or small, God sees all of His creatures and cares for all of His Creation.
- (*Point to the poster, and read it aloud to the children.*) Big or small, God cares for all. Can you say that with me? (*Have the children repeat the phrase with you.*) Big or small, God cares for all.
- God cares for the little birds. He sees everything that happens to them. He knows exactly what they need, and He takes care of them. If God cares about the little birds, we know that God cares for us too. We are even more valuable to Him than the birds.
- The Bible tells us about how much God cares for us and loves us. (*Hold up your Bible.*)
- Did you know there are billions of people who live in this world? Even so, God knows each of us by name. He knows my name, and He knows your name.
- The Bible also tells us that God even knows the number of hairs that are on our heads. I want you to try to count how many hairs are on your head. Ready? Go ahead. Try to count them. (*Allow children to try to count the hairs on their heads. Start counting your own hairs one by one. Stop after counting several hairs.*) Can you count them all? There are just too many! I do not think we could ever do it, but God knows the exact number of hairs on each of our heads.
- The Bible also tells us that God knows every tear we have ever cried. When we are sad, we might cry and have tears go down our cheeks. God knows about every tear you have ever cried. God knows why we were sad and how we felt.
- God knows about all those things. He knows every thought we think even before we think it. He knows every word we say even before we say it. He knows everything we do.

- Now, why do you think God would care about these little details, like how many hairs are on our head or how many tears we have cried? Why would it matter to Him? (*Allow children to respond.*) Yes, because God cares for us. He cares for all of His Creation, because He is the One who made us, and He loves us!
- If God knows and cares about all those things, like the number of hairs on our head, then God cares about other things too. He cares about things that make us sad, things that make us upset, things that make us happy, and things that make us worried.
- I have some paper plates representing different faces to show various ways we might feel. (*Hold up one of the plates as an example to show the children.*) I will need some helpers to hold these plates. The rest of us will try to guess how the person is feeling.
- (*Ask for two volunteers to hold up the happy face plates. Give each of the volunteers one plate. Have them hold the plates up in front of their own faces and stand facing the rest of the group.*)
- How do these faces look like they are feeling? (*Allow children to respond.*) Yes, they look like they are happy. (*Collect the plates from the two volunteers, and have them sit back down with the rest of the group.*)
- God cares when we are happy. What are some things that might make us happy? (*Allow children to respond. Share some things that make you feel happy, if you are comfortable doing so.*)
- (*Do the same with the sad, angry, and worried face plates. Choose two different volunteers each time to hold up the plates. Then, allow children to share experiences that cause them to feel each emotion. Share your own experiences as well.*)
- We can talk to God about all those things. We can talk to God and pray no matter how we feel. God wants us to pray to Him about anything, whether it seems like a big thing or a small thing. Remember, big or small, God cares for all. (*Point to the poster on the wall as you read the phrase.*)
- Our Bible memory verse for today is 1 Peter 5:7. (*Read the entire verse aloud to the children as you point to the words on today's memory verse poster.*)
- No matter how we feel, we can talk to God about it and know that He cares for us. If we are worried, upset, or scared about something, we can talk to God about it. If we are happy, we can talk to God about it. If we are sad, we can talk to God about it. We can talk to God anytime and anywhere and about anything. Even if we do not say the words aloud, God still hears us. We can trust that God cares for us very much. He loves you very much. God knows exactly what we need, so we can trust that He cares for us. God wants us to love Him, obey Him, and trust that He cares for us.
- Before we leave, let's pray and tell God thank You for caring for us so much.
- (*If time allows, let children share prayer requests with the group if they would like. Lead the group in prayer to close.*)

DAY 3: Bible Lesson

Let All Creation Praise the Lord

Supplies Needed:

- Variety of rocks
- Palm branches
- Coats, jackets, or sweaters
- Paper
- Music player (e.g., CD or mp3 player)
- Rhythm instruments
- Chocolate rocks, popping candy rocks, or rock candy pieces

Preparation:

- This lesson is based on Psalm 19:1-4; Luke 19:28-40; and Romans 1:20. Read these passages to help you prepare to teach this lesson.
- Collect some rocks for the children to observe during the lesson. Try to have a variety of colors, textures, and sizes. If possible, use a rock identification kit, as this will provide several different kinds of interesting rocks for the children to look at and will also provide a guide to help identify the rocks by name.
- For this lesson, you will need some palm leaves. You can find or purchase real palm leaves, use artificial ones, or make your own using green construction paper.
- On blank paper, make signs by writing one of God's characteristics on each paper. Examples include: God is great, God is powerful, God is loving, and God is faithful.
- Choose one or more praise songs to play at the conclusion of the lesson.

Teaching Instructions:

- Welcome back, campers! At Camp Genesis, we have been learning about God's Creation. One thing that God created is rocks.
- I have some rocks I want you to take a look at today. We will pass them around and let everyone observe them up close. (We are not going to throw the rocks, because they could hurt someone if we did.)

- *(Give a rock to each child, and allow time for observation. Have the children pass the rocks around, so everyone has a chance to see and touch each different rock.)*
- What do you notice about these rocks? How are they the same, and how are they different? Raise your hand if you would like to share one observation you made about these rocks. *(Allow children to share their responses. Prompt the children by asking about the texture, weight, size, color, etc.)*
- I have one more question for you about these rocks. While you were looking at them, did anyone hear any of the rocks talk? Did they say anything? *(Allow children to respond.)*
- Have you ever heard a rock talk, shout, or say anything? *(Allow children to respond.)*
- I have never heard a rock talk, but the Bible tells us about a time when the rocks may have something to say.
- *(Open your Bible as you begin telling the Bible story.)* This story is in the book of Luke in our Bibles, which is in the New Testament. It tells about a time when Jesus, God's Son, was riding into a city called Jerusalem. This was just about a week before Jesus was going to die on the cross and then come back to life.
- Jesus was riding on a donkey into the city of Jerusalem. There was a large crowd of people, and they were shouting and praising God. They were throwing down their coats on the road and making a path on which Jesus could ride. They had palm branches from the trees, and they were shouting praises to God. Some people also placed branches on the road to line the way for Jesus. They were treating Jesus like a king, and they were kind of making a "red carpet" for Him to ride on.
- We are going to make a path at the front of our classroom like the one those people made for Jesus that day. *(Give each child a palm branch or a coat, and let the children place them down on the ground in a path at the front of the classroom.)*
- This crowd was so excited to praise God, but there were also some people there that day who did not like what was happening. In fact, these people wanted the crowds to stop praising God. These people went to Jesus and told Him to tell the people who were praising God to stop it!
- But it was good for the people to praise God. God deserves our praise.
- When these people told Jesus to tell the others to stop their praise, Jesus told them that even if the people kept quiet and did not praise God, even the rocks would cry out and praise God!
- Can you imagine? If the people stopped shouting praises to God, even the rocks would start crying out and praising God. God deserves praise, and if people do not praise Him, then I guess the rocks would have to do it.
- Now, I know that we have never really heard rocks say anything, but they could; nothing is impossible for God. But even if we do not hear the rocks speak any words, they do praise God in their own way. In fact, all of Creation brings God praise.

- *(Ask for volunteers to hold up the signs naming God's characteristics as you talk about each one.)*
- When we look at the rocks and other things God created, like the trees, the oceans, or the stars, it helps us understand just how **great** God really is. We know that God is **powerful**, because He created all of these things. We know that God is **loving**, because He cares for His Creation. We know that God is **faithful**, like the sun that comes up every morning. Everyone in the world can see how great God is when they look at all the things He has made. *(Discuss other characteristics of God and how we see those demonstrated in our world. Additional examples include: God is wise, God is holy, God is sovereign, God is eternal, God is patient, God is merciful, and God is good.)*
- The rocks and all of God's Creation help teach us about God and bring Him praise. The trees wave their leaves, the rocks cry out, and the skies proclaim how great God is. God is the Creator and the King of all Creation. He is the One who made it all!
- When we think about how great God is and how much He loves us and cares for His Creation, we just want to praise Him too! We want to praise God in everything we do.
- *(Review today's Bible memory verse.)*
- God has given us the special privilege of having a mouth and breath that we can use to praise God, so we are going to praise God right now with a song.
- *(Turn on the praise music, and encourage children to sing and clap along with the song. You could also allow the children to use rhythm instruments during the song or pick up a palm leaf and wave it with the music. If there is extra time, play another praise song or repeat the same song.)*
- *(Give each child a couple of chocolate rocks, some popping candy rocks, or some rock candy as they are leaving your station. Let the children know that these rocks are OK to eat because they are made of candy, but we do not eat other types of rocks.)*

DAY 4: Bible Lesson
Growing Like Jesus

Supplies Needed:

- Four plants or flowers
- Green and brown paper
- Construction paper
- Tape
- Bible

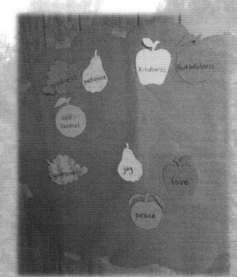

Preparation:

- This lesson is based on Psalm 1:1-6; Matthew 7:15-20; Luke 6:43-45; John 15:1-17; 1 Corinthians 3:5-9; Galatians 5:13-26; and Colossians 1:9-14. Read these passages to help you prepare to teach this lesson.
- You will need four plants for this lesson to help illustrate what plants need to grow. Several days in advance of your lesson, place one of the plants in a dark closet where it will not receive any sunlight, but continue to water it regularly. Place a second plant in a dark closet, but do not water it. Place a third plant in a sunny place, but do not give it any water. Make sure it is in a location that will not receive any rainfall either. Place the fourth plant in a location that will receive plenty of sunlight, and water it regularly. When it is time for this lesson, place the plants on a table in your classroom.
- Using green and brown paper, make four large "trees" to tape on the wall of your classroom. They should be fairly large, but short enough for children to reach the green area of the trees.
- Using various colors of construction paper, cut out circles to look like fruit, or use a die-cut machine to make fruit shapes. On each piece of fruit, write one of the fruit of the Spirit listed in today's Bible memory verse (love, joy, peace, forbearance, kindness, goodness, faithfulness, gentleness, and self-control). The children will tape these on the tree during today's lesson. You can remove the fruit from the tree after each group leaves your station, or you can make four sets of fruit – one for each group's tree.

Teaching Instructions:

- Welcome back, campers! Today, we are learning that God makes things grow.
- God is the One who created plants, trees, flowers, and all living things. We know that these things grow by looking at them over time. The grass in our yard gets taller, and we have to mow the lawn. Trees bear fruit, and their leaves change colors. Flowers start off as tiny seeds and then bloom into beautiful blossoms. All of these changes show us that God is making those plants and trees grow.
- What types of things do plants and trees need to grow? (*Allow children to respond.*) They need sunlight and water. They get nutrients from the soil. If a tree is healthy and has everything it needs, it will grow and bear good fruit.
- I would like you to take a look at these plants that have been growing. (*Point to each plant on the table as you describe it.*) This first plant received plenty of sunlight and water. This second plant was in a sunny spot, but did not get any water. The third plant got plenty of water, but it was in a dark room and did not get any sunlight. The fourth plant did not receive water or sunlight.
- Which of these plants looks the healthiest? Stand up on your carpet square if you think this plant is the healthiest. (*Point to the first plant, and allow children to respond. Have those children sit down, and then ask the same question while pointing to the second, third, and then the fourth plant.*)
- Why do you think this plant is the healthiest? (*Allow children to respond about the plant they chose.*)
- The first plant received everything it needed to help it grow big and strong – water, sunlight, and nutrients. The other plants did not have everything they needed to help them grow. They were missing something very important.
- God is the One who created the plants and trees and makes them grow. He also created the water, sun, and soil that plants need.
- God gives *us* the things we need to help us grow as well. Not only does God help us grow taller, older, and smarter, but He also wants to help us grow to be more like Jesus.
- Just as water and sunlight help plants and trees grow, there are certain things that help us grow to be more like Jesus. When we read our Bibles, pray, and come to church, God can use those things to help us grow to be more like Jesus. Without these things, we would not be able to grow as much in our faith.
- We are going to sing a song about how God helps us grow more like Jesus. Stand up on your carpet square, and we will sing it together.
- (*Lead the children in singing "Read Your Bible, Pray Every Day." When the song says "shrink," gradually crouch down lower to the ground. When the song says "grow," gradually stand up taller.*)

- "Read Your Bible, Pray Every Day" Lyrics:

    If you neglect your Bible, forget to pray, forget to pray, forget to pray,
    If you neglect your Bible, forget to pray, then you'll shrink, shrink, shrink.
    Then you'll shrink, shrink, shrink. Then you'll shrink, shrink, shrink.
    If you neglect your Bible, forget to pray, then you'll shrink, shrink, shrink.

    But if you read your Bible, pray every day, pray every day, pray every day,
    If you read your Bible, pray every day, then you'll grow, grow, grow.
    Then you'll grow, grow, grow. Then you'll grow, grow, grow.
    If you read your Bible, pray every day, then you'll grow, grow, grow!

- By reading the Bible, we get to know God and His ways better. We can read God's Word to help us know how to obey Him. We can also pray and ask God to help us grow more like Jesus. Praying is when we communicate with God.
- On our own, we cannot live a perfect life. No, Jesus is the only One who ever lived a perfect life. But we can ask God to forgive our sins and ask Jesus to be our Savior. God wants to help us grow to be more like Jesus. God gives us His Holy Spirit to live in us to help us obey Him. We should trust God and obey Him, because He always knows what is best for us.
- We have to rely on God to give us what we need to help us grow. Just as these plants need water and sunlight to grow, so also we need to continue reading our Bibles and praying in order to help us grow more like Jesus.
- If we trust God and have His Spirit living in us, then we can grow like a strong, healthy tree. (*Point to one of the trees on the wall.*) Healthy trees have good fruit growing on them.
- When we have God's Spirit living in us, we will have good fruit in our lives too. We are not going to start growing fruit like apples and oranges off our arms or anything, but we will have good things growing in our lives.
- In fact, our Bible memory verse for today talks about this. When we believe in Jesus and His Spirit lives in us, then we will have the fruit of God's Spirit growing in our lives. The fruit of the Spirit is love, joy, peace, forbearance, kindness, goodness, faithfulness, gentleness, and self-control. (*Point to the Bible memory verse sign on the wall, and have the children say the verse with you.*)
- God will help these good things grow in our lives as we trust and obey Him. These are the types of characteristics Jesus had in His life and the types of characteristics God wants to grow in our lives too as He helps us to grow more like Jesus.
- (*Hold up the first paper fruit that says "love." Ask for a volunteer to come tape the fruit on the tree.*) God helps us to **love** Him and other people. What are some ways that we can show love to other people? (*Allow children to respond.*)

- (*Do the same with the other paper fruits. Hold up each one, and have a volunteer tape it on the tree. Then, discuss that fruit of the Spirit with the children.*)
- God helps us to have **joy**. How can people tell if we have God's joy in our lives?
- God helps us to have **peace**. What does it mean to have God's peace?
- God helps us to have **forbearance**, which is another word for **patience**. What does it mean to be patient?
- God helps **kindness** to grow in our lives. What are some ways we can be kind?
- God helps **goodness** to grow in our lives. What does goodness mean?
- God helps **faithfulness** to grow in our lives. What does it mean to be a faithful person?
- God helps **gentleness** grow in our lives. What does it mean to be gentle?
- God helps us to have **self-control**. What does it mean to have self-control?
- When we trust in Jesus as our Savior and His Holy Spirit lives in us, God helps all of this good fruit of the Spirit grow in our lives.
- Let's pray and ask God to help us grow to be more like Jesus and have these good things grow in our lives. (*Lead the children in prayer.*)
- (*If there is extra time, sing "Read Your Bible, Pray Every Day" with the children again.*)

DAY 5: Bible Lesson

The First Family

Supplies Needed:

- Construction paper
- Fruity snacks
- Printer paper
- Crayons, markers, or colored pencils

Preparation:

- This lesson is based on Genesis 2:5-4:16 and Mark 12:28-30. Read these passages to help you prepare to teach this lesson.
- The family night carnival will take place during the last half of Camp Genesis today. Because of this, there will only be two station rotations. See the alternate rotation schedule for day five for more details. Two groups will be combined into one larger group for each rotation, so you will have twice as many students in your classroom during one rotation as you have had on previous days. Rearrange your classroom's seating arrangement as necessary to accommodate for this larger group.
- Remove the fruit of the Spirit shapes from the trees on your classroom wall used in yesterday's lesson. Tape some plain construction paper circles on the trees to look like fruit as a decoration for this lesson about the Garden of Eden.
- Cut out two large hearts from red construction paper. On one heart, write "Love God." On the other heart, write "Love Others." Tape these hearts on the wall of your classroom near the trees.
- Choose a fruity snack that you will give to the children during the lesson today. You can use real fruit cut into small pieces. (Check with the snack station leaders for any leftovers.) As an alternative, you could use small fruit chews or fruit-flavored candy. Be sure to check the children's registration forms for any food allergies.
- Make copies of the printable resource for this lesson, which features today's Bible memory verse. This is available on our blog at http://smallpublishing.wordpress.com.
- To add another dimension to your story, have two adult or teen actors portray Adam and Eve. They can act out their parts such as eating the fruit and hiding among the trees. They should leave the room when they are kicked out of the garden in the story.

Teaching Instructions:

- Welcome back, campers. Can you believe today is our last day of Camp Genesis? We have had an exciting journey so far, and today, as we learn that God created our families, we are going to look back at the very first family God created.
- First, I would like you to look at these two hearts on the wall. (*Point to the hearts on the wall.*) In the Bible, Jesus said that the two most important commands are to love God and to love one another.
- As you hear about the first family God created, I want you to listen to see if you think they did those two things. Did they love God, and did they love each other?
- The very first person God created was a man named Adam. God had taken some of the dust of the ground and formed Adam. God breathed into the man, and he became a living human being.
- Later, when Adam was sleeping, God took one of Adam's ribs, and from that rib, God created the very first woman. Her name was Eve. Adam and Eve were the first people God created. They were married, and they lived in a beautiful place called the Garden of Eden. It was a perfect paradise. They walked and talked with God. He loved them, and they loved Him.
- In the garden, there were all kinds of trees with fruit growing on them. Here is a sample of what that might have tasted like, although I am sure the fruit from the Garden of Eden tasted even better than what we have here today. (*Give each child a couple of pieces of fruit or fruit snacks to eat.*)
- God had given them lots of good fruit to eat, but He also gave them one important command. There was one tree in the middle of the garden called the tree of the knowledge of good and evil. (*Point to one of the trees decorating the wall in the middle of the classroom.*) God said that they could eat from any tree in the garden except that one. They were not to eat from that tree or something very bad would happen.
- One day, a serpent, which is like a snake, said to Eve, "Did God really say that you cannot eat from any of the trees in the garden?"
- Eve told the serpent, "We can eat from any of the trees, just not the one in the middle of the garden. If we eat from that tree, something very bad will happen."
- "Oh, nothing bad will happen," the serpent said to her.
- Eve looked at the fruit on the tree in the middle of the garden. It did look pretty good, but she knew God had said not to eat it. Still, it looked really good. Eve knew God's command, but the fruit was still very enticing. What do you think Eve did? (*Allow children to respond.*)
- Eve did eat some of the fruit from the tree that God had said not to eat. She gave some to Adam, and he ate it too. Later, when they heard God walking in the garden, Adam and Eve hid among the trees.

- God called to Adam, "Where are you?"
- Adam told God, "I was scared, so I hid."
- "Did you eat from the tree I told you not to eat from?" God asked.
- "Well, Eve gave me some and I ate it," Adam said.
- God asked Eve, "What have you done?"
- "Well, the serpent tricked me, and I ate it," Eve replied.
- Adam and Eve were trying to blame others, but they had made the choice. They knew God's command, but they had still disobeyed Him. That was the very first sin. Now, they deserved to be punished. Adam and Eve were kicked out of the garden. Things changed after that. People were separated from God. Before that, there was no sickness or death, no pain or suffering, but the world was no longer perfect. Even the ground came under a curse. Our world has never been the same because of that bad choice Adam and Eve made.
- (*Point to the heart on the wall that says "Love God."*) Do you think Adam and Eve did a good job of loving God with all their heart? (*Allow children to respond.*) If they loved God, they should have trusted Him and obeyed His command. Instead, they chose to go their own way and not obey God's command. Do you think God was happy that they disobeyed? Why or why not? (*Allow children to respond.*)
- Later, Adam and Eve became parents. They had two sons named Cain and Abel. Abel loved God. Cain was jealous of his brother and hurt him and treated him very badly.
- (*Point to the heart on the wall that says "Love Others."*) Do you think Cain did a good job of loving his brother? (*Allow children to respond.*)
- God has given us these commands for our good, because God knows that families are most joyful when they love Him and love each other. But this first family did not set a very good example for us, did they? They disobeyed, and there were consequences.
- If we are honest, though, the members of this first family are not the only ones who have ever disobeyed God. God knows that it is best for us when we love Him and love each other, but sometimes we don't do that, do we? Sometimes we disobey God like Adam and Eve did. Maybe it is not about eating a piece of fruit, but it could be something else like telling a lie, stealing something, saying something mean or hurtful to someone, disobeying our parents, or doing something else that is not done out of love for God or others. That is called sin, and we have all done it.
- The good news is that even when Adam and Eve disobeyed and sinned, God still loved them, and God still loves us too, even when we disobey Him.
- You see, even way back then, God had a plan, and He made a promise. Because God loves us so much, God was going to send a Savior to take the punishment for human sins. This Savior would forgive our sins and help us to love. God kept that promise, and He sent Jesus to be the Savior. Jesus lived a perfect life on earth. He is the only one who has never sinned – not even once.

- But Jesus died on the cross to take the punishment for our sins. He did not deserve to be punished, but He did it for all of us. He was willing to sacrifice Himself for us.
- After Jesus died, God brought Him back to life. He did not stay dead; He rose again.
- When we believe and trust in Jesus as our Savior, He forgives our sins and will help us to love God and love others like we should. He has also given us the promise that all who believe in Him will live with God forever someday in a perfect paradise, like Adam and Eve did in the beginning. We all need Jesus – all of us and all of our families – to help us to love God and each other.
- I would like to pray with you, and if you would like to ask Jesus to be your Savior, to take away your sins, and to help you to love God and love others, we can ask Him right now. Let's close our eyes, bow our heads, fold our hands, and pray together.
- *(Lead the children in prayer. A sample prayer is given below.)*
- Dear God, Thank You for creating our families. Thank You for creating each one of us. We confess that we have not always obeyed You as we should. We have not always loved You and loved others like we should. Please forgive us for our sins against You. We are sorry. We believe that You sent Jesus to be our Savior. Thank You that He died on the cross to take the punishment for our sins and that He rose again from the dead and lives forever. We ask Jesus to be our Savior and pray that You would help us to obey You and follow You. Help us to love You and love each other as we should. Thank You that You always know what is best for us and for our families. Help our families to follow You and love You every day. In Jesus' Name, amen.
- God created that first family, and God created our families as well. He made dads and moms, grandpas and grandmas, uncles and aunts, brothers and sisters, and sons and daughters. All of our families are unique. That means they are one of a kind. However, we all have some things in common too. God made our families, God loves our families, and God wants our families to love Him and love each other.
- *(Review today's Bible memory verse.)* Serving the Lord means that we follow and obey His ways. It means that we love Him and share His love with others.
- I am going to give each of you a piece of paper, and on that paper, I want you to draw one way that you will show your love for God and for your family. You might draw a picture of your family praying before dinner or a picture of you helping your younger sibling. You are going to draw a picture, but then I want you to take this home and actually do whatever it is that you draw. We are not going to just draw it and then forget about it. Go home and do it! If you draw your family praying together, do it! Maybe you could lead the prayer. If you draw your family going to church together, do it! Ask them if you can all come this weekend. If you draw yourself helping a younger sibling, do it! Go and help them. We want to put our love into action.
- *(Give each child one copy of the Day 5 printable resource, along with crayons, markers, or colored pencils. If you have extra time, allow children to share their drawings with the group.)*

Notes:

Notes:

Camp Genesis:

Exploring God's Creation

Adventure Trail

Game Leader's Guide

Small Publishing | Belleview, Florida

To the Game Leader:

In Mark 10:14, Jesus said, "Let the little children come to me, and do not hinder them, for the kingdom of God belongs to such as these."

As a Camp Genesis volunteer, you're living out that very command. You have the great privilege and responsibility of helping children discover the truth of who God is and what He has done and of leading them to a faith-filled relationship with Him.

Please take a moment in prayer and ask God to prepare your heart as you seek to serve Him and His children. Remember, your job is to be a model of God's love.

When you're ready, turn the page and get ready to lead kids on an exciting adventure in God's Word as we discover His amazing Creation and get to know our great Creator!

*"The heavens declare the glory of God;
the skies proclaim the work of his hands."*
(Psalm 19:1)

Adventure Trail

Games

Day 1: Days of Creation Relay

Children will participate in a relay race with objects representing each day of Creation.

Day 2: Creation Scavenger Hunt

Children will explore the details of God's Creation as they search to find various objects on their checklists.

Day 3: Pavement Praise

Children will use sidewalk chalk to write praise messages to God and draw pictures of reasons to praise Him.

Day 4: Good Fruit/Bad Fruit

Children will separate balloons with good characteristics from the bad ones, representing the good and bad fruit that can grow in our lives.

Day 5: Family Night Carnival

Children will invite their families to join them for a closing carnival, complete with games and activities celebrating God's Creation.

Supply List
for Adventure Trail Games

(See the teaching instructions for the individual days for more details about supplies.)

Day 1 – Days of Creation Relay:
- ☐ Two small objects to represent each day of Creation such as:
  - ☐ Bright-colored papers with the word "light"
  - ☐ White bath puffs
  - ☐ Artificial flowers, leaves, or fruit
  - ☐ Yellow balls
  - ☐ Stuffed bird and fish
  - ☐ Stuffed animal and doll
- ☐ Six folding chairs
- ☐ Large tarp, mat, or blanket
- ☐ Paper
- ☐ Tape
- ☐ Starting line (plastic cones, tape, etc.)
- ☐ Non-transparent bag

Day 2 – Creation Scavenger Hunt:
- ☐ Copies of scavenger hunt list
- ☐ Crayons
- ☐ Pieces of cardboard (slightly larger than a piece of typing paper)
- ☐ Clothespins

Day 3 – Pavement Praise:
- ☐ Sidewalk chalk
- ☐ Large pavement area
- ☐ Plastic cones
- ☐ Old towels
- ☐ Hand wipes

Day 4 – Good Fruit/Bad Fruit:
- ☐ Balloons
- ☐ Foam boards
- ☐ Tape
- ☐ Two baskets
- ☐ Two tarps
- ☐ Starting line (cones, tape, etc.)

Day 5 – Family Night Carnival:
- ☐ See the Day 5 instructions for a complete list of supplies needed for each carnival game.

Introduction
for the Game Leader

General Instructions for the Game Leader:

- Choose a spacious area outside for your game station. Mark clear boundaries and ensure that the children know they are to stay within those boundaries. Encourage children to follow safety procedures when walking outside. Be extra cautious if crossing parking lots or streets. Have children stay with a buddy when outside.

- When children are outdoors, they are able to discover and explore God's Creation firsthand. As you follow the activity plans detailed on the following pages, be sure to also take advantage of teachable moments and point out things that God created to help reinforce what the children are learning at Camp Genesis. For example, be on the lookout for a bird nest you can show the children, or pause for a moment and encourage children to listen quietly for bugs chirping in the distance.
- All of the games and activities can take place outside. However, in case of inclement weather, have an alternate indoor location reserved for the game station if needed. Below are some daily adaptations if the activities are moved indoors:
    - Day 1 – The relay race can take place as planned indoors or outdoors, as long as there is an ample amount of room for children to move and run. For safety, be sure any furniture or other objects are moved out of the playing area. If you would rather the children not run indoors (especially if you have hard floors), you can add a fun twist to the game by requiring the children to crawl like a crab, hop like a frog, or move like another animal during the relay race.
    - Day 2 – If you are unable to hold the scavenger hunt outdoors, hide pictures of the objects or, when possible, the real objects themselves inside. Have the children search for these pictures or objects indoors.

- Day 3 – If weather necessitates moving indoors or you do not have a safe pavement area or sidewalk large enough to complete this activity, cut large lengths of roll paper and tape the paper to the floor of a spacious room indoors. Allow the children to make their praise drawings and messages using markers, colored pencils, or crayons on these large pieces of paper. Modify the teaching instructions, calling the activity Paper Praise.
- Day 4 – This game can take place indoors or outdoors, as long as there is an ample amount of room for children to move and run. For safety, be sure any furniture or other objects are moved out of the playing area. If you do not want the children to run while indoors, encourage the children to pretend to fly like a bird or move like another animal as they take their turns.
- Day 5 – The carnival can take place indoors or outdoors. An indoor setting may actually be preferred if your church has enough rooms and areas for the games to take place. As families move throughout the various areas where games are being held, they would have an informal "tour" of your ministry facilities, and this may help them to become more comfortable with the church environment. An indoor carnival may also be desirable since the supplies needed for the many games taking place at once would be more difficult to move inside quickly in the case of a pop-up shower or storm. If the carnival is held outdoors, be sure to account for the wind, and tie down decorations or have weights for objects that may be apt to fly away.

- During each station rotation, gather the children together in a huddle around you or have them sit on the ground in front of you before beginning the game. During this time, introduce the day's game or activity to the children and talk about how it connects with the day's theme, as detailed in the teaching instructions on the following pages. At the conclusion of the game time, gather the group together again. Discuss the game they just played and its connection to what they are learning at Camp Genesis. Use this time to reinforce the main teaching points of the day, and review the daily Bible memory verses as well. You can also pray with the children to conclude your time together before they rotate to the next station.
- Be sure to provide lots of encouragement while the children are participating in the games and activities, and encourage the children to cheer each other on as well. Some children may feel insecure about their physical abilities. Do not force a child to participate in an activity. Take an active part in the games if you are able, and encourage the other leaders to do the same. Your example may help encourage children to participate and enjoy the activities with the group.

DAY 1: Game

Days of Creation Relay

Supplies Needed:

- Two small objects to represent each day of Creation
    - Suggestions:
    - Day 1: bright-colored papers with the word "light" written on them
    - Day 2: white bath puffs (clouds)
    - Day 3: artificial flowers, leaves, or fruit
    - Day 4: yellow balls (sun and moon)
    - Day 5: stuffed bird and fish
    - Day 6: stuffed animal and doll
- Six folding chairs
- Large tarp, mat, or blanket
- Paper
- Tape
- Starting line (plastic cones, tape, etc.)
- Non-transparent bag

Preparation:

- Designate a starting line for the teams, marking it with a line of tape, plastic cones, or another indicator to help ensure that team members stay behind the starting line until it is their turn.
- A distance away from the starting line, set up the six chairs in a straight line, so that the front of each chair can be seen from the starting line.
- Write the numbers 1 through 6 on pieces of paper (one number per paper). Tape one of these signs to each of the chairs, starting with number 1 on the far left chair (when viewed from the starting line).
- Lay the tarp out on the ground behind the chairs. Label the tarp with the number 7.
- Place all of the objects representing God's Creation in a non-transparent bag, so the children cannot see the objects until you take them out of the bag.

Teaching Instructions:

- Welcome to the Adventure Trail at Camp Genesis! This is where we will enjoy some fun games and activities together at camp as we explore all of the wonderful and awesome things God made!
- God is so powerful that He created our entire world. Did you know that God created the whole world in seven days? (Actually six, because God rested on the seventh day.)
- Do you remember our Bible memory verse? It is from Genesis 1:1. It says, "In the beginning God created the heavens and the earth." *(Have children repeat it with you.)*
- On the first day, it was very dark. But God said, "Let there be light," and there was light. God spoke and created the light. He separated the light from the darkness. He called the light "day," and He called the darkness "night." I have something in my bag to represent the light that God created. *(Take the objects representing the light out of your bag and show them to the children.)*
- On the second day, God created the sky. *(Take the objects representing clouds out of your bag and show them to the children.)* These represent the clouds in the sky God created.
- On the third day, God separated the oceans from the dry ground. He made plants and trees to grow on the land. This includes the flowers, fruit trees, and leaves. *(Take the objects representing this day out of your bag and show them to the children.)*
- On the fourth day, God created some lights for the sky. The lights that God made are called the sun, the moon, and the stars. *(Take the objects representing the sun and moon out of your bag and show them to the children.)*
- On the fifth day, God created the birds that fly in the sky as well as all of the creatures in the oceans. *(Take the objects representing this day out of your bag and show them to the children.)* The sky and the oceans were full of living creatures now.
- On the sixth day, God created lots of different kinds of animals. He made the livestock, the wild animals, and the creatures that move along the ground. *(Take the stuffed animal out of your bag and show it to the children.)* On the same day that God made the animals (the sixth day), God also made something very special. He made a human being! The very first person that God made was named Adam. *(Take the doll out of your bag and show him to the children.)*
- By the seventh day, God had finished all of the work He had been doing. He had made light, the sky, oceans, the ground, plants, trees, the sun, the moon, stars, birds, fish, animals, and a human. So, on the seventh day, God rested from His work. He did not create anything on the seventh day. Instead, He rested and enjoyed everything that He had already created. He saw that it was very good.
- Today, we are going to play a game called the "Days of Creation Relay." I want you to listen carefully for instructions so you will know how to play the game.

- We have some chairs and a tarp set up with the numbers one through seven on them. They represent each day of Creation. *(Point these out to the children.)*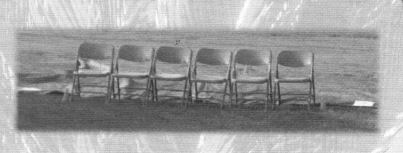
- For this game, there will be two teams. The first person on each team has to take the object representing the light God created, run down, and place it on the chair marked with the number 1, since God made light on the first day.
- Then that player will run back and tag the second person on his or her team. The second person on each team will then take the cloud, run down, place the object on chair 2, and run back.
- We will continue taking turns like that for days three through six. *(Review what object corresponds with each day.)*
- There is no item for the seventh day. Do you remember what God created on the seventh day? *(Allow children to respond.)* God rested on the seventh day, because He had finished the work He had been doing. So, after the sixth person on each team places his or her object on the correct chair, that person will run back to the starting line. Then your entire team will run to the seventh day tarp and sit down on it to show that God rested from His work on the seventh day. Your team cannot start running toward the tarp until the sixth player has returned to the starting line.
- The first team to have all its members sit down on the seventh day tarp is the winner!
- *(Divide the children into two teams.)* I need both teams to line up behind the starting line, and I am going to give each team the objects you will need. *(Lay the objects out for each team near the starting line. The objects should be laid out in order according to the day on which God created each item. Keep each team's set of objects separate.)*
- When I say go, the first member of each team can pick up the first object and start running toward the first chair. On your mark, get set, go!

Special Note for the Leader:

- Some team members may have to take more than one turn, if there are less than six players per team. If there is a very large group of children, you may need to form more than two teams and add additional objects as needed.
- Younger children may enjoy the activity more if it is not considered a race. Instead of having teams, you could have all the members of the youngest group work together as one team. Assist the children in taking turns running objects down to the correct chairs. Once all of the objects have been taken to the correct chairs, have all of the children run down and sit on the seventh day tarp. Play again if there is time.

DAY 2: Game
Creation Scavenger Hunt

Supplies Needed:

- Copies of printable scavenger hunt list
- Crayons
- Pieces of cardboard
  (slightly larger than a piece of typing paper)
- Clothespins

Preparation:

- Choose a large area that will be used for children to explore during this activity, and decide where the boundaries will be.
- Scout out your area and discover what special items from God's Creation are found in your specific location. The scavenger hunt list provided is used as a general example, but you can create a modified list to fit your unique location if you desire.
- As you survey your location in preparation for the scavenger hunt, be on the lookout for any trouble spots in the area (e.g., poison ivy, large holes, roads, etc.), and warn children to stay away from these hazards.
- Make copies of the printable scavenger hunt list so you have enough for each child. This is available for download on our blog at http://smallpublishing.wordpress.com.
- Use the clothespins to clip each list to a piece of cardboard, making a "clipboard" for the children to use during the scavenger hunt.

Teaching Instructions:

- I hope you are having a great time at Camp Genesis as we have been exploring God's Creation. There are so many wonderful things that God has made. Sometimes we do not take the time to enjoy them all, but today we are going to go on a scavenger hunt as we explore the details of God's Creation.
- I have a list for each of you that tells the things you will be trying to find on this Creation Scavenger Hunt. *(Give each child a clipboard with a list attached.)*

- Look at the first part of the list. You are going to use your eyes to look and see if you can spot these things in God's Creation. The list says to look for a pinecone, bird, piece of tree bark, small twig, tree, flower, bird nest, leaf, spider web, bug, nut or acorn, rock, squirrel, worm, feather, seed, lizard, butterfly, cloud, and sun.
- There are also some things on your list you will need to listen for with your ears. (These are below the line on your list.) You will try to listen and see if you hear these things: a bird chirping, bug buzzing, leaf crunching, and wind blowing.
- When you see or hear something on the list, put a check in the box beside that object. For example, if I see a flower, then I am going to mark the box beside the word and picture of the flower. *(Demonstrate for the children how to do this.)*
- You probably will <u>not</u> find all of the items on the list, and that is OK. They may not all be found right here where we will be looking. Your goal is to try to find as many as you can. When time is up, we will all come back together and share some of the neat things we found as we explored God's Creation.
- While we are exploring, we do not want to disturb any of the things we find. That means we will not pick the flowers, we will not touch any bird feathers, and we will not collect acorns to take with us. We just want to observe with our eyes and ears.
- Here are the boundaries for our scavenger hunt. *(Point out the specific boundaries of your location to the children.)* We are going to do our exploring in this area, and we will not go beyond these boundaries. *(Point out any hazardous spots to the children as well, and warn them to stay away from these areas.)*
- You will each need a buddy or two to stay with during the scavenger hunt. *(Assist the children in finding partners with whom to explore.)*
- Here are crayons for you to use to mark your list. *(Give each child one crayon.)*
- *(Give the children some type of signal when it is nearing the time to start rotating to the next station. Gather the children back together and talk about some of the things they found on their scavenger hunt. Talk with them about how God cares for all of His Creation, even the little things. God created the entire universe, but He knows the number of hairs on our heads and cares for us. Pray with the children and thank God for His wonderful Creation.)*

Special Note for the Leader:

- Be sure that you have enough adult leaders to supervise the children during this activity. If your area is very large or has dangerous spots, you may want to require that the children remain with an adult leader during the scavenger hunt. This would be especially important for the youngest groups of children.

Creation Scavenger Hunt

- ☐ Pinecone
- ☐ Bird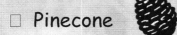
- ☐ Piece of tree bark
- ☐ Small twig
- ☐ Tree
- ☐ Flower
- ☐ Bird nest
- ☐ Leaf
- ☐ Spider web
- ☐ Bug

- ☐ Nut or acorn
- ☐ Rock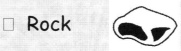
- ☐ Squirrel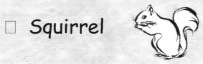
- ☐ Worm
- ☐ Feather
- ☐ Seed
- ☐ Lizard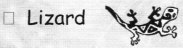
- ☐ Butterfly
- ☐ Cloud
- ☐ Sun

- ☐ Bird chirping
- ☐ Bug buzzing

- ☐ Leaf crunching
- ☐ Wind blowing

DAY 3: Game

Pavement Praise

Supplies Needed:

- Sidewalk chalk
- Large pavement area
- Plastic cones
- Old towels
- Hand wipes

Preparation:

- Choose a large area outside, such as a parking lot or sidewalk, where children will be able to safely sit and draw on the pavement. (If you do not have such a space available outside, see the "Introduction for the Game Leader" pages for a modified indoor activity.) You may want to use plastic cones to block off the area from vehicles. Be sure to have enough adult leaders on hand to safely supervise the children and watch for any motorists entering the area.
- If possible, have a separate area marked off for each group, so each new group of children will have a clean canvas of pavement on which to make their drawings. Also, instead of bringing out all of the chalk for the first group, save back some of the chalk, so that each group will have some new full-size pieces of chalk to use.
- Draw a few things on the pavement ahead of time (such as a heart, cross, and sun) to give the children some ideas.
- Have some old towels available for the children to sit on, since black pavement may get very hot in the summer sun.

Teaching Instructions:

- Today, we have been talking about praising God, our great Creator, and declaring how good He is. For today's activity, we are going to give Him some Pavement Praise!

- When I pass out the chalk, you can use it to draw your own reasons to praise God. Maybe you want to praise God for something He created. You could draw a picture of the thing God created. You could also write words and messages about why You want to praise God. There are lots of reasons we can praise God.
- I want to praise God because He loves me, so I drew a heart. *(Point out your sample drawings to the children.)* I want to praise God for creating the sunshine, so I drew the sun. I also want to praise God because Jesus died for me on the cross and then God brought Jesus back to life, so I drew a cross.
- Remember, we are only using our chalk to draw or write reasons we want to praise God.
- *(While the children are making their drawings on the pavement, walk around and talk with them about the things they are drawing and why they want to praise God.)*
- *(Before children rotate to the next station, have them use a wipe to clean the chalk off their hands.)*

DAY 4: Game

Good Fruit/Bad Fruit

Supplies Needed:

- Balloons
- Foam boards
- Tape
- Two baskets
- Two tarps
- Starting line (tape, plastic cones, etc.)

Preparation:

- Design two healthy-looking "good" trees and two dead-looking "bad" trees out of foam board (one good and one bad tree per team). Stand them against a wall, or tape them to something sturdy like chairs so they will stand up securely during the game.
- For each team, blow up nine balloons of one color and nine balloons of a different color. (You will need 144 balloons total – 72 of each color.)
- Write one of the following nine characteristics on each "good" (Color A) balloon:
    1. Love
    2. Joy
    3. Peace
    4. Patience
    5. Kindness
    6. Goodness
    7. Faithfulness
    8. Gentleness
    9. Self-control
- Write one of the following nine characteristics on each "bad" (Color B) balloon:
    1. Selfishness
    2. Rudeness
    3. Hate
    4. Jealousy
    5. Disobedience
    6. Dishonesty
    7. Meanness
    8. Bitterness
    9. Greed
- Tape each team's set of nine "good" balloons to their "good" tree. Tape each team's set of nine "bad" balloons to their "bad" tree. Do this again after each station rotation.
- Designate a starting line a distance away from the trees and mark with tape or cones.
- Place a basket at the starting line for each team.
- Place a tarp on the ground near each set of trees where children will stomp on the "bad" balloons.

Teaching Instructions:

- Welcome back to the Adventure Trail! Today's game is called "Good Fruit/Bad Fruit." You will see that we have some trees we are going to use as part of our game. Let's take a closer look at these trees. *(Have the children gather around near one set of trees and sit down.)*
- What do you notice about these trees? How are they similar and how are they different? *(Allow the children to respond.)*
- We might call one tree a *good* tree and one a *bad* tree. The good tree looks very healthy and alive. The bad tree looks very unhealthy, even dead.
- We can tell if a tree is good or bad if we look at the fruit growing on it. If a tree is good, it is going to have good fruit that grows from it, but if a tree is bad, its fruit will be bad too. *(See Matthew 12:33.)*
- Let's look at some of the things that are written on these balloon fruits. Here is what is growing on the good tree. *(Read the words written on the balloons taped to the good tree. Explain the meaning of any words with which the children may not be familiar.)* There is no bad fruit on this tree.
- Let's see what is growing on the bad tree. *(Read the words written on the balloons taped to the bad tree. Explain the meaning of any words with which the children may not be familiar.)* This is all bad fruit. There is no good fruit on this tree at all.
- God wants to help us grow to be like the good tree. When we trust in Jesus as our Savior, God makes good things grow in our lives – good fruit like love, joy, peace, patience, kindness, goodness, faithfulness, gentleness, and self-control. This is the way Jesus lived, and God wants to help us grow to be more like Jesus. When we have God's Spirit living in us, He helps us to be more loving and kind, more patient and forgiving and faithful. Our hearts will be full of God's love and He will help us to love others, to be joyful, and to have His peace.
- But if we do not trust in Jesus, we are like the bad tree. On our own, we might have things growing in our lives like hate, selfishness, disobedience, and rudeness. People who do not trust in Jesus are like the bad tree. They do not love God, and they do not listen to God, so God cannot help them to love others like they should.
- If we have these bad things in our lives, we need to ask God to forgive us. God can help us grow to be more like Jesus and have good fruit in our lives, like the good tree.
- God does not want us to be like the bad tree. He wants to help us grow like a good tree. We cannot do it on our own, but with God's power, we can! Nothing is impossible for God. God can help us to grow and be like Jesus.
- For this game, there are going to be two teams. Your team's job is to get rid of all the bad fruit and collect all of your team's good fruit in a basket.

- The members of your team will take turns running to your team's trees. When it is your turn, you will run down to one of your trees and grab a piece of fruit off the tree. If it is from the *good* tree, you will run back to the starting line and put the balloon in your team's basket. If you grab a balloon from the *bad* tree, you will put the balloon on the tarp and stomp on it to pop it. After it pops, run back to the starting line and tag the next player on your team. That person will then run down and grab one piece of fruit off one of the trees and either bring it back to your team's basket (if it is a good fruit) or stomp on it (if it is a bad fruit).
- Remember, on your turn, you will only grab one piece of fruit. Then it will be the next player's turn. The first team to get rid of all their bad fruit and collect all their good fruit in the basket is the winner!
- Do you have any questions before we begin? *(Allow the children to respond.)*
- *(Divide the children into two teams. Point out to each team which trees belong to their team.)*
- When I say go, the first player on each team should run down and choose a piece of fruit from one of your trees. Are you ready? On your mark, get set, go!
- *(After the game, you can talk with the children more about how God wants to help us grow to be more like Jesus and have good fruit in our lives. You could also pray with the children that God would help us be like a good tree.)*

Special Note for the Leader:

- Adult leaders should clean up all of the broken balloon pieces after each group plays the game. Balloon pieces can be a choking hazard to young children, so do not allow children to pick up any broken pieces.
- If you use latex balloons, check the children's registration forms for any latex allergies.
- It is suggested to use water balloons for this game because they are thinner and easier to pop and also smaller than regular balloons. However, fill them with air, not water, for this game.

DAY 5: Game

Family Night Carnival

Special Note for the Leader:

- Take note of the different schedule for day five of Camp Genesis. The Adventure Trail game station will not take place in a normal station rotation. Instead, the family night carnival will be held during the last part of this day's programming. Various carnival games and activities relating to the theme of God's Creation will be set up for children and families to enjoy. Below are instructions and supply lists for games and activity stations that can be set up at the carnival. Coordinate with the director of Camp Genesis as you help prepare for the carnival.

Preparation:

- Decide on the number of activities you want to offer during the carnival, and recruit volunteers to run the games. Group leaders, craft helpers, and the Bible lesson teacher can run games at the carnival, since they will not have their normal responsibilities during this time. Try also to recruit additional adult or teen volunteers from your congregation who may not be able to help during the entire five days of camp, but may be able to volunteer for a couple of hours at the carnival. If possible, let the volunteers who have children participating in Camp Genesis be free to enjoy the activities with their family for at least part of the carnival.
- Choose a location where each game will be held. Decide whether the carnival will be held indoors or outdoors. If you hold the carnival inside your church, families would have an informal "tour" of your ministry facilities as they move throughout the various areas where games are being held. This may help them to become more comfortable with the church environment.
- Gather all supplies needed for each game, and assign a volunteer to each activity. Be sure these leaders understand their assignments and the game rules. Carnival leaders will need to take their places while the children are finishing the closing ceremony.
- Prepare bags with small prizes and candy to be given to each child following the carnival. Prepare a few extras to give to children who may not have attended Camp Genesis but may be present for the family night carnival (e.g., younger siblings).

Supplies Needed:

- **Falling Leaves:** green and brown paper, construction paper, marker, tape, blindfold
- **Days of Creation Bucket Toss:** seven buckets, objects from Day 1's game
- **Sunny or Cloudy Throw:** yellow paper (or chalk), masking tape, cotton balls
- **Fishing Game:** cardstock, magnet pieces, kiddie pool, yarn, unsharpened pencil, bucket, blindfold
- **Butterfly Catch:** butterfly net, coffee filters, clothespins
- **Rainbow Ring Toss:** empty soda bottles, food coloring, masking tape, diving rings
- **Seed Toss:** seed trays (or flower pots), masking tape, seeds, cup
- **Stick Drop:** sticks/twigs, containers (e.g., cans, jars, bottles, etc.)
- **Mystery Objects:** rock, pinecone, stick, leaf, seashell, acorn, tree bark, flower, non-transparent containers (e.g., margarine tubs, whipped topping containers, etc.)
- **Creation Beanbag Toss:** cardboard, box cutter, masking tape, beanbags (or other small, soft objects)
- **Tic Tac Toe:** poster board, five pinecones and five rocks (or other objects)
- **Duck Pond:** plastic tub, water, plastic ducks
- **Animal Treasure Hunt:** plastic tub, packing peanuts, plastic toy animals (or other small items)
- **Coconut Bowl:** green construction paper, empty two-liter bottles, masking tape, round brown ball
- **Bird Flight:** hula hoop, white cotton material, yarn, paper, crayons, masking tape
- **Family Portraits:** camera, backdrop, props, paper, pen or pencil
- **Family Faces Snack:** see snack leader's guide for supplies needed
- Prize bags

Instructions:

- **Falling Leaves:** This game is similar to "Pin the Tail on the Donkey." Create a tree on the wall out of green and brown paper (or use the pretend trees from Day 4 or Day 5's lesson or Day 4's game). You could have several trees of different heights. Cut some small leaf shapes out of construction paper. With a marker, write the child's name on one of the leaves, and put a piece of tape on the back of the leaf. Hand the leaf to the child. Blindfold the child and turn him or her around once. Then, have the child try to place the leaf on the tree.

- **Days of Creation Bucket Toss:** Place seven buckets in a line and label with the numbers 1 through 7. Have children try to toss an object in each bucket that corresponds with what God created on each day. (You can use the same objects used in the game for Day 1 of Camp Genesis or find other objects that represent each day of Creation.) Remind the children that there will not be an object to toss in the Day 7 bucket, since God rested from His work on that day.
- **Sunny or Cloudy Throw:** Cut a large circle out of yellow paper, along with several long thin strips of yellow paper. Tape these on the floor to look like a sun with rays. (If this activity is taking place outside, you could draw the sun on the ground using chalk instead.) With tape, mark a line on the ground a distance away from the sun for children to stand behind. Vary the distance based on children's ages or heights. Have the children toss cotton balls, and try to land these "clouds" on the sun or its rays.
- **Fishing Game:** Cut fish shapes out of cardstock, and attach a magnet piece to each fish. Scatter the fish in the (dry) pool. Tie a length of yarn to the end of an unsharpened pencil, and attach a magnet piece to the other end of the string. The child should hold the pencil, trying to "catch" the fish by hooking the magnet on the end of the string to one of the magnets on the fish. Place  a bucket beside the pool, and once the fish has been lifted out of the pool, the child should place the fish in the bucket. Children can be challenged to catch all of the fish in the pool or to catch as many as possible in a certain amount of time. For a more difficult challenge, blindfold the child, turn him or her around once, and then let the child go fishing.
- **Butterfly Catch:** Create "butterflies" by folding a coffee filter like a fan and attaching it to the middle of a clothespin. With tape, mark a line on the ground for children to stand behind a distance away from where the butterfly net will be. Vary the distance based on children's ages or heights. Hold out the butterfly net. Children should gently toss the butterflies and try to land them in the net.
- **Rainbow Ring Toss:** Fill empty soda bottles with water. Add a few drops of food coloring to each bottle, so each one is a different color. Screw the lids on tightly and stand them on the ground. With tape, mark a line on the ground a distance away from the bottles for children to stand behind. Vary the distance based on children's ages or heights. Give the children some rings to throw, and have them try to ring them around the bottles.

- **Seed Toss:** Place the seed trays on the ground. (Small flower pots could also be used instead of seed trays.) With tape, mark a line on the ground a distance away from the trays for children to stand behind. Vary the distance based on children's ages or heights. Give the child a cup with a few sunflower or pumpkin seeds. The child should stand behind the line and toss the seeds one at a time at the seed tray, aiming to land the seeds in the openings of the tray. For a more difficult challenge, have the children aim for the four corners of the tray.
- **Stick Drop:** Collect containers of various sizes. Set the containers on the ground. Have the child stand an arm length away from the container, extend his or her arm, and try to drop the stick in the container. Children should stand up tall and may not bend over. Use containers with a wider mouth for younger children, and use containers with a smaller hole to give older children more of a challenge. You can also use different sized sticks to make the game more or less challenging.
- **Mystery Objects:** Collect objects from God's Creation such as the ones suggested. Place one object in each non-transparent container, so children will not see what is inside. (The containers should all look the same.) Have a list or pictures of the objects, and have children try to guess which object is inside each container. Children may shake the containers and feel their weight, but they may not look inside. After children make their guesses, open the containers to reveal if they were correct. Replace the objects, close the lids, and move the containers around after each child takes a turn so the next participant will not know which object is in which container.
- **Creation Beanbag Toss:** Cut some holes out of a sturdy piece of cardboard, and decorate it with a Creation theme (e.g., underwater, animals, trees and fruit, outer space, flowers, etc.). Stand the board diagonally against a wall. (You could also cut holes out of one side of a cardboard box instead of using a flat piece of cardboard.) With tape, mark a line on the ground a distance away from the board for children to stand behind. Vary the distance based on children's ages or heights. Give the children beanbags, and have them try to toss them through the holes.
- **Tic-Tac-Toe:** Draw a large tic-tac-toe grid on poster board. (You can make several boards so several pairs can play at the same time.) One player will use rocks, and the other will use pinecones, instead of the traditional X's and O's. Players take turns placing one of their objects in one square on the board. The first player to get three in a row of his or her objects (horizontally, vertically, or diagonally) is the winner.

- **Duck Pond:** Fill a plastic tub or container with a small amount of water, and place a set of plastic ducks in the water. Each duck should have the number 1, 2, or 3 written on the bottom. Children should choose a duck out of the pond and look at the number on the bottom of the duck. The numbers on the ducks correspond to various tasks the children must complete. For example, if children pull out a duck with the number 1, they should name something that God created. If children choose a duck that has the number 2, they should tell one reason they want to praise God. If the duck shows the number 3, children should tell one thing that is special about their family.
- **Animal Treasure Hunt:** Fill a plastic tub or container with packing peanuts. Bury the toy animals throughout the packing peanuts. Ask the child to find a specific object hidden inside, and see how fast the child can find it. After the item has been found, bury the item back in the packing peanuts and let the next participant take a turn.
- **Coconut Bowl:** Cut several oval shapes out of green construction paper to make "leaves." Tape one end of each leaf to the lid of an empty two-liter bottle to create a "tree." Make several trees and stand them up on the ground like bowling pins. With tape, mark a line on the ground a distance away from the trees for children to stand behind. Vary the distance based on children's ages or heights. Give children a round brown ball to represent a "coconut," and have them roll the ball and try to knock down the trees.
- **Bird Flight:** Attach white cotton material around the hula hoop to make it look like a cloud. Use yarn to hang the hoop so it is suspended mid-air. Fold some paper airplanes and decorate them to look like birds. Allow the children to make their own birds if they would like. With tape, mark a line on the ground a distance away from the hoop for children to stand behind. Vary the distance based on children's ages or heights. Children should throw the bird to help it fly through the cloud. For safety, be sure no one is standing behind or near the hula hoop when birds are in flight. The birds should be left at this station and not taken to other stations. If children want to keep theirs, write their names on them and give them back following the carnival.
- **Family Portraits:** Have a station set up where families can get their pictures taken. Set up a backdrop and have family groups sit or stand together in front of it. Take at least one serious pose, and then allow the families to use various props to take some silly pictures together. Have families write down their email or mailing addresses and send them a photo after Camp Genesis.
- **Family Faces Snack:** The day's snack will be set up as one station during the carnival. Families will decorate crackers using various toppings to represent the faces of family members. See the snack leader's guide for detailed instructions.

Notes:

Notes:

Camp Genesis:

Exploring

God's Creation

The Canteen

Snack Leader's Guide

Small Publishing | Belleview, Florida

To the Snack Leader:

In Mark 10:14, Jesus said, "Let the little children come to me, and do not hinder them, for the kingdom of God belongs to such as these."

As a Camp Genesis volunteer, you're living out that very command. You have the great privilege and responsibility of helping children discover the truth of who God is and what He has done and of leading them to a faith-filled relationship with Him.

Please take a moment in prayer and ask God to prepare your heart as you seek to serve Him and His children. Remember, your job is to be a model of God's love.

When you're ready, turn the page and get ready to lead kids on an exciting adventure in God's Word as we discover His amazing Creation and get to know our great Creator!

"The heavens declare the glory of God;
the skies proclaim the work of his hands."
(Psalm 19:1)

The Canteen
Snacks

Day 1: Creation Cups
Children will enjoy cups of God's Creation including gelatin ocean water, dirt pudding, and animal crackers.

Day 2: Edible Bird Nests
Children will create their own edible bird nests, reminding them that God cares for us even more than a mother bird cares for her baby birds.

Day 3: Praise Him S'more
Children will enjoy a favorite camp snack as they praise God and then praise Him s'more.

Day 4: Seed-bearing Fruit
Children will enjoy a snack of apple slices and observe different types of fruits and their seeds.

Day 5: Family Faces
During the closing carnival, children and families will decorate crackers to represent members of their families.

Supply List
for The Canteen Snacks

(See the teaching instructions for the individual days for more details about supplies.)

All Days:
- ☐ Drinks
- ☐ Cups
- ☐ Napkins
- ☐ Plates or bowls
- ☐ Trash can
- ☐ Peanut butter
- ☐ Jelly
- ☐ Bread
- ☐ Hand sanitizer
- ☐ Bible memory verse posters

Day 1 – Creation Cups:
- ☐ Clear plastic cups
- ☐ Blue gelatin mix
- ☐ Gummy fish
- ☐ Chocolate pudding
- ☐ Chocolate sandwich cookies
- ☐ Gummy worms
- ☐ Animal crackers
- ☐ Spoons

Day 2 – Edible Bird Nests:
- ☐ Small bowls
- ☐ Spoons
- ☐ Plastic zip-close bags
- ☐ Peanut butter
- ☐ Pretzel sticks
- ☐ Potato sticks
- ☐ Licorice strings
- ☐ Jelly beans
- ☐ Pictures of birds and nests

Day 3 – Praise Him S'more:
- ☐ Graham crackers
- ☐ Chocolate bars
- ☐ Large marshmallows

Day 4 – Seed-bearing Fruit:
- ☐ Apples
- ☐ Various other fruits with seeds
- ☐ Foam plates or trays
- ☐ Plastic wrap
- ☐ Peanut butter or caramel dip

Day 5 – Family Faces:
- ☐ Round crackers
- ☐ Spreads such as:
    - Peanut butter
    - Chocolate hazelnut spread
    - Spreadable cheese
    - Cream cheese
    - Marshmallow crème
- ☐ Toppings such as:
    - Shredded cheese
    - Crushed crackers
    - Crushed cookies
    - Shredded vegetables
    - Chocolate shavings
    - Shredded coconut
    - Licorice
    - Baking chips
    - Candy pieces
    - Raisins

Introduction
for the Snack Leader

Daily Supplies Needed in the Snack Station:

- Drinks
- Cups
- Napkins
- Plates or bowls
- Trash can
- Peanut butter
- Jelly
- Bread
- Hand sanitizer
- Bible memory verse posters

General Instructions for the Snack Leader:

- Be aware of food allergies. These should be listed on the children's registration forms (or you may need to ask the children if they are allergic to any foods or if there are certain foods they are not allowed to have). Peanut allergies can be common among children, so be especially cautious with the snacks that contain peanut butter as an ingredient. If children have a known food allergy, check with the child's parents or guardians for safe alternative ingredients. Cream cheese, chocolate hazelnut spread, spreadable cheese, pudding, jam or preserves, yogurt, sunflower seed butter, marshmallow crème, icing, whipped cream, and hummus are all spreadable foods that may be able to serve as substitutes for peanut butter in the snack recipes.
- Many children may arrive without having eaten lunch or supper and may be hungry. They will be better prepared to learn if their needs are met and their stomachs are satisfied. To help meet this need, prepare peanut butter and jelly sandwiches each day to offer the children. These can be served in addition to the regular daily snack. (Again, be aware of any food allergies the children may have.)

- Coordinate with the volunteers in charge of registration to get the number of children and leaders in attendance each day in each group, so you will know how many snacks to prepare for each rotation.
- In addition to snacks for the children, prepare snacks for the leaders and helpers, if there are enough supplies. If you or another volunteer in your station has time, you may want to deliver snacks to the other station leaders (games, crafts, and lessons). Be sure the snack station volunteers take a break and enjoy the snacks too! However, make sure there are enough snacks for all the children before allowing leaders or helpers to consume any.
- Pray with the children each day before serving the snacks and drinks. You can lead the children in prayer or see if one or more of the children would like to pray aloud for the group.
- Have children wash their hands, or have a bottle of hand sanitizer available and encourage the children to use some before they eat. Many of the groups will have just come from the game station, so this will help keep germs away!
- If children finish their snacks early, have them practice their daily Bible memory verses. Print and hang the daily Bible memory verse posters in the snack station. Read these to the children, and have them practice saying them to their friends or leaders. See if they can recite the verses without looking. Review previous days' verses as well.
- You could also set up a "photo booth" area in the snack station as an extra time activity. Choose a plain wall for children to stand in front of, or hang up a sheet or tablecloth as a backdrop. You could even have some fun props available, and have children pose and get their pictures taken.
- Encourage children to take a bathroom break if needed before they leave your station. This is a good time and location for a bathroom break, and this will hopefully help limit the interruptions in other stations.

DAY 1: Snack

Creation Cups

Supplies Needed:

- Clear plastic cups
- Blue gelatin mix
- Gummy fish
- Chocolate pudding
- Chocolate sandwich cookies
- Gummy worms
- Animal crackers
- Spoons

Special Note for the Leader:

- Each child should receive three Creation Cups (one of each kind). Since children will be receiving three separate snacks, each Creation Cup should be prepared in small serving sizes (i.e., the cup needs only to be filled halfway or less).

Preparation for Creation Cup #1:

- This snack will need to be prepared a day in advance, in order to give the gelatin time to set.
- Prepare the blue gelatin according to the instructions on the package.
- Pour some gelatin water in each plastic cup, so that the cup is about a third full.
- Allow the gelatin to set up in the refrigerator.
- After the gelatin has set, push a couple gummy fish gently into the top of the gelatin in each cup.
- Prepare some additional blue gelatin water, and pour some more gelatin water into each cup until the cups are about half full.
- Place the gelatin cups back into the refrigerator to allow them to set.

Preparation for Creation Cup #2:

- Prepare the chocolate pudding according to the instructions on the package.
- Fill each plastic cup about half full with pudding.
- Crush the chocolate cookies and sprinkle a layer of crushed cookies on top of the pudding in each cup.
- Gently press a couple of gummy worms through the cookie layer and partway into the pudding so parts of the worms are still visible on top of the cookie layer in each cup.

Preparation for Creation Cup #3:

- Place some animal crackers in each cup so the cups are about one-third to one-half full.

Teaching Instructions:

- Welcome to the Canteen at Camp Genesis! This is where you will come to enjoy snacks each day at camp. During our time at Camp Genesis, we are going to be exploring God's Creation, the things God made.
- God created the heavens and the earth. God created the light. God created the ground. God created the oceans. God created the plants and the flowers and the trees. God created the sky and the sun and the moon and the stars. God created the fish in the sea. God created the birds in the air. God created the wild animals and the livestock and the creatures that move along the ground. God also created people. God made me and He made you. God made all of these things.
- For our snack today, we are going to enjoy some of the things that God made.
- You will each receive three Creation Cups. One cup shows the ocean that God made and the fish that God made. *(Hold up one cup of gelatin ocean water for the children to see.)* Another cup represents the ground that God made and even some worms that God made. *(Hold up one cup of dirt pudding.)* The third cup has animal crackers that represent all the different kinds of wild animals and livestock that God created. *(Hold up one cup of animal crackers.)*
- Before we eat, let's pray and tell God thank You for all that He has created and for providing this food for us today. *(Pray.)*
- *(After praying, distribute one cup of gelatin ocean water, one cup of dirt pudding, and one cup of animal crackers to each child, along with a spoon, napkin, and drink. Each child should also be offered a peanut butter and jelly sandwich.)*

DAY 2: Snack

Edible Bird Nests

Supplies Needed:

- Small bowls
- Spoons
- Plastic zip-close bags
- Peanut butter
- Pretzel sticks
- Potato sticks
- Licorice strings
- Jelly beans
- Pictures of birds and nests

Preparation:

- Prepare individual servings of each ingredient for the children by doing the following. Place a couple spoonfuls of peanut butter in each bowl (one per child). Put a serving of pretzel sticks, potato sticks, and licorice, along with two or three jelly beans, in each plastic zip-close bag (one per child).
- You may want to make a sample bird nest snack to give the children a visual idea of how to build their own bird nests.
- Gather some pictures of birds and nests. Search online and print out some pictures, check out a library book, or take your own photos if you see a real bird nest.

Teaching Instructions:

- Do you remember on what day God created the birds? *(Allow children to respond.)* It was on day five!
- Have you ever seen a bird nest before? *(Allow the children to respond.)*
- A mother bird builds a nest where she will lay her eggs. After she lays the eggs, she sits on the eggs and keeps them warm until they are ready to hatch. After the eggs hatch, the mother bird helps protect the baby birds, and she gives them food to eat such as insects, worms, or seeds.

- The baby birds rely on their mother to take care of them and give them the food they need. *(Show the children some pictures of birds and their nests.)*
- Just as the baby birds rely on their mother, we have to rely on God to take care of us. God knows what we need. God wants us to trust Him, obey Him, and put Him first. God will give us everything we need.
- God is the One who made the animals and plants grow that provide us with food to eat, and God gives us water to drink. When we eat and drink, God gives us energy and strength. God gives people the ability to work and make good food to eat.
- God wants us to trust that He cares for us. He hears us when we talk to Him and cry out to Him, like a mother bird hears her baby birds when they call.
- Today, you are going to make your own bird nest to remind you that God cares for us even more than a mother bird cares for her baby birds. That is a lot! God loves us very much!
- When a mother bird starts to build a nest, she looks for items she can use. What do you think she might use to build her nest? *(Allow the children to respond.)*
- She will gather twigs, sticks, straw, grass, hair, fur, strings, or anything else she can find that might be good to use in her nest. Some birds use mud in their nests too.
- We are going to build our bird nests inside a bowl to help them keep their shape. Your bowl will have some peanut butter in it to help hold your nest together.
- You will also receive one of these bags of supplies. *(Hold up one bag of ingredients.)* This is what you will use to build your nest. Each bag has some pretzel sticks, potato sticks, and licorice you can use.
- When you receive your supplies, use your spoon to smear the peanut butter around the inside of your bowl and then start building. Stick some of your pretzel sticks, potato sticks, and licorice to the peanut butter inside your bowl. *(Show the sample snack you made, and model how to place the ingredients around the bowl.)*
- Your bag also contains a few jelly beans. After you have built your nest, you can put the jelly beans in your nest to look like bird eggs.
- When you are all done, you can use your spoon to enjoy eating the pretend bird nest.
- Before we start building, let's pray and tell God thank You for caring for us and thank You for this food. *(Pray.)*
- *(After praying, distribute a bowl with peanut butter, a spoon, a bag of ingredients, a napkin, and a drink to each child. Each child should also be offered a peanut butter and jelly sandwich.)*

Special Note for the Leader:

- Be sure to check the children's registration forms for any food allergies. See the "Introduction for the Snack Leader" pages for ideas about alternate ingredients if needed.

DAY 3: Snack

Praise Him S'more

Supplies Needed:

- Graham crackers
- Chocolate bars
- Large marshmallows

Preparation:

- Break the graham crackers in half (if they are not already pre-split in half).
- Break the chocolate bars apart into individual pieces.
- To make each snack, place one graham cracker face down.
- Place one chocolate piece on top of the graham cracker.
- Place a marshmallow on top of the chocolate.
- Microwave for about 7 to 15 seconds so the marshmallow will begin to melt.
- After removing from the microwave, press another graham cracker on top of the marshmallow.
- The s'mores do not need to be made too far in advance, since they take less than a minute to microwave and are good to eat when they are warm.

Teaching Instructions:

- Today, we have an ooey, gooey, yummy snack for you. This is a favorite snack to eat at camp. It is called a s'more. It is made with graham crackers, chocolate, and marshmallows. It is sticky and delicious!
- Do you know why these are called s'mores? Because after you eat one, you want some more (s'more)!
- You know, it is the same way when I think about praising God. I praise Him, and then I just want to praise Him s'more!
- What are some reasons you want to praise God? (*Let children share their responses.*)
- Can we think of s'more reasons to praise Him? (*Let children share their responses.*)
- What are s'more reasons you want to praise Him? (*Continue asking the children this, and let them share their responses.*)

- Those are some wonderful reasons to praise God. Let's praise Him s'more by praying and telling Him thank You for our food today. *(Pray.)*
- *(Give each child <u>one</u> s'more to start. Since they will probably want some more, you may allow them to come back for one more if they want.)*
- *(Each child should also be offered a drink and a peanut butter and jelly sandwich.)*

Special Note for the Leader:

- Be sure to check the children's registration forms for any food allergies.
- Some children may be allergic to or may not like chocolate or marshmallow. In this case, they may request a specially made s'more without one of the ingredients.

DAY 4: Snack

Seed-bearing Fruit

Supplies Needed:

- Apples
- Various other fruits with seeds
- Foam plates or trays
- Plastic wrap
- Peanut butter or caramel dip

Preparation:

- Cut a few slices of various types of fruit (e.g., lemon, orange, kiwi, etc.). Place the slices on foam plates or trays (only one type of fruit per tray). Cover the trays with plastic wrap. These will be for display purposes only.
- Wash and slice apples for children to eat. (This should not be done *too* far in advance, or the apples may begin to turn brown. Use lemon juice if needed.)

Teaching Instructions:

- Do you remember on what day of Creation God made the plants and trees? *(Allow children to respond.)* It was on day three!
- When God made the very first plants and trees, He created them to produce seeds.
- The trees grew and produced fruit, and that fruit had seeds inside. Each type of plant and tree had a different kind of seed. Each kind of seed was unique.
- God made apple trees that grew apples with apple seeds in them. God made lemon trees that grew lemons with lemon seeds inside them. God made orange trees that grew oranges with orange seeds inside them.
- One of those seeds can fall to the ground and be planted in the dirt. The seed gets water and sunshine, and then God makes it grow. It takes a while for it to grow, but God makes it grow into a big tree. Then that new tree grows more fruit that has seeds in it. Those seeds may get planted in the ground, and God helps new trees to grow. The cycle continues like that.

- God made many different kinds of fruit, in many different colors. Each kind of fruit has a different type of seed. They all look different.
- I have some fruits for you to look at today. *(One at a time, hold up the trays displaying the different types of fruit slices. Tell the children the name of each type of fruit.)*
- I will pass these trays around for you to look at and observe. We are going to look with our eyes, but we are not going to take off the plastic wrap. I want you to see if you can spot the seeds in each type of fruit. Notice how the seeds of each type of fruit look different.
- *(Pass the fruit slice trays around to the children and allow them to observe the various kinds of fruit and seeds.)*
- Do you see the seeds inside? Just as each type of fruit looks different, their seeds look different as well.
- Some fruits have lots of little seeds in them. Other fruits may have only a few seeds, or maybe even just one "pit" inside them.
- Have you ever seen a seed in a fruit you have eaten? *(Allow the children to respond.)* We eat the fruit, but for most fruits, we do not eat the seeds.
- Today, we are going to enjoy some tasty apple slices. These apples grew from a tree that God made. That big tree started as just a little apple seed. The seed was planted in the ground, it received water and sunshine, and God helped it grow into an apple tree!
- God helps us people grow too, just as He helps the little seeds grow into a big tree.
- God gave us this good fruit to enjoy. Fruit is healthy and can help us grow big and strong.
- Before we eat, let's pray and tell God thank You for all of the wonderful trees and fruits with seeds He created and for helping us grow too. *(Pray.)*
- *(After praying, distribute the apple slices for children to eat. You may also choose to give the children a spoonful of peanut butter or caramel in which to dip their apples. Each child should also be offered a drink and a peanut butter and jelly sandwich.)*
- *(While the children are eating, you may want to discuss with them:* What is your favorite fruit that God made?*)*

Special Note for the Leader:

- Be sure to check the children's registration forms for any food allergies. Serve an alternate fruit or dip if necessary.

DAY 5: Snack

Family Faces

Supplies Needed:

- Round crackers
- Spreads (e.g., peanut butter, chocolate hazelnut spread, spreadable cheese, cream cheese, marshmallow crème)
- Toppings (e.g., shredded cheese, crushed crackers or cookies, shredded vegetables, chocolate shavings, shredded coconut, licorice, baking chips, candy pieces, or raisins)

Preparation:

- The last half of the last day of Camp Genesis will be devoted to the family night carnival. **Due to the carnival, this day's snack will not take place in a normal station rotation.** The snack will be set up as an activity station only during the carnival time, and families and children may come and go as they please. This snack will be for children as well as their family members who attend the carnival, so keep this in mind when determining how many snacks to prepare.
- Choose several different spreadable ingredients to put on the crackers. Before families arrive, spread one of the ingredients on each cracker, and place the crackers on trays. Have a variety of choices available to represent different skin tones.
- Choose toppings to represent the hair, mouth, eyes, and nose. Try to have a variety of colors available to represent different hair colors and eye colors. To represent different hair colors, your selection of toppings might include shredded cheese, crushed crackers or cookies, shredded vegetables, chocolate shavings, and shredded coconut. Licorice can be used for the mouth, and baking chips, candy pieces, and raisins can be used for the eyes and nose. Place these toppings in bowls along with a spoon for each.

Teaching Instructions:

- Today, you are going to decorate crackers to look like your family! God made our families. Each family member is unique and special, so each cracker will look unique.
- We have toppings available to represent different colors of skin, eyes, and hair.
- Choose a couple of crackers from the trays to start and put them on your plate.
- Then, you may choose the toppings you would like to use to decorate your crackers. *(Offer suggestions to the children as to which toppings could be used to represent various features, but let them be creative.)*
- Use the spoons to take the toppings out of the bowls, and pour them on your plate. *(For cleanliness, encourage children not to put their fingers in the bowls that will be shared by all. Refill the bowls as needed throughout the night.)*
- Then, you can sit down and place the toppings on your crackers to look like a face. Show your family the crackers you decorated, and tell them who each one represents!

Notes:

Notes:

Camp Genesis:
Exploring God's Creation

Creation Crafts

Craft Leader's Guide

Small Publishing | Belleview, Florida

To the Craft Leader:

In Mark 10:14, Jesus said, "Let the little children come to me, and do not hinder them, for the kingdom of God belongs to such as these."

As a Camp Genesis volunteer, you're living out that very command. You have the great privilege and responsibility of helping children discover the truth of who God is and what He has done and of leading them to a faith-filled relationship with Him.

Please take a moment in prayer and ask God to prepare your heart as you seek to serve Him and His children. Remember, your job is to be a model of God's love.

When you're ready, turn the page and get ready to lead kids on an exciting adventure in God's Word as we discover His amazing Creation and get to know our great Creator!

"The heavens declare the glory of God;
the skies proclaim the work of his hands."
(Psalm 19:1)

Creation Crafts

Crafts

Day 1: Creation Collages

Children will use a variety of materials to design collages representing things God created.

Day 2: Recycled Birdfeeders

Children will turn old juice cartons into birdfeeders, reminding them of God's care for all of His Creation.

Day 3: Praise Rocks

Children will decorate pet rocks to remind them that we should praise God, our Creator.

Day 4: Plant People

Children will create their own plant people by planting grass seed to grow as hair, reminding them that God makes us grow.

Day 5: Stick Figure Families

Children will use twigs to represent their relatives, making their own unique stick figure family displays.

Supply List
for Creation Crafts

(See the teaching instructions for the individual days for more details about supplies.)

All Days:
- ☐ Smocks
- ☐ Permanent marker
- ☐ Hand wipes
- ☐ Bible memory verse posters
- ☐ Large cardboard trays

Day 1 – Creation Collages:
- ☐ Paper or foam plates or trays
- ☐ Various collage items to represent God's Creation
- ☐ Printer paper
- ☐ White glue
- ☐ Paintbrushes

Day 2 – Recycled Birdfeeders:
- ☐ Clean, empty 59-64 oz. drink cartons
- ☐ Masking tape
- ☐ Colored pencils
- ☐ Twine
- ☐ Birdseed
- ☐ Small paper bags

Day 3 – Praise Rocks:
- ☐ Large, smooth rocks
- ☐ Acrylic paint
- ☐ Paintbrushes
- ☐ White glue
- ☐ Wiggle eyes
- ☐ Yarn
- ☐ Pom-poms
- ☐ Paper plates

Day 4 – Plant People:
- ☐ Large foam cups
- ☐ Markers
- ☐ Potting soil
- ☐ Plastic spoons
- ☐ Grass seed
- ☐ Misting bottles with water
- ☐ Card stock
- ☐ Plastic drinking straws or craft sticks
- ☐ Small paper bags

Day 5 – Stick Figure Families:
- ☐ Sticks/twigs
- ☐ Wiggle eyes
- ☐ White glue
- ☐ Green floral foam blocks
- ☐ Card stock
- ☐ Hot glue guns
- ☐ Paper plates

Introduction
for the Craft Leader

Daily Supplies Needed in the Craft Station:

- Smocks
- Permanent marker
- Hand wipes
- Bible memory verse posters
- Large cardboard trays

General Instructions for the Craft Leader:

- Create a sample of each day's craft to give children a visual idea of what they will be making. However, encourage children to use their creativity to make their own unique projects and not just copy the samples.
- You may want to have the children wear smocks while completing their craft projects, so they will not get their clothes dirty.
- Have a leader write the children's names on their projects with a permanent marker.
- Encourage children to clean up their own areas when they have finished their projects (e.g., throw away trash, put supplies in their proper places, etc.). Have plenty of wipes available for children to use to clean their hands before rotating to the next station.
- If children finish their crafts early, have them practice their daily Bible memory verses. Have posters hanging in the craft station with the daily verses printed on them. Read these to the children, and have them practice saying them to their friends or leaders. See if they can recite the verses without looking. Review previous days' verses as well.
- Designate a place in your station to put each group's crafts when they are complete. After the last station rotation, carry the crafts to an area near the exits where children will be picked up at the end of the day. (Collect large cardboard trays from grocery stores, and use these trays to carry several craft projects at one time.) The children should be reminded in the closing each day to pick up their crafts before they go home. Have adult helpers assist you in distributing the crafts as children leave. If crafts need time to dry, keep them at your station until the next day of camp, and give them to the children when they leave at the end of that day.

DAY 1: Craft
Creation Collages

Supplies Needed:

- Paper or foam plates or trays
- Various items to represent God's Creation (see "Preparation" section below for ideas)
- Printer paper
- White glue
- Paintbrushes

Preparation:

- Gather supplies that children can use for their collages. A variety of supplies should be made available for children to use in order to spark their creativity. Some supplies that may be used include stamps, stickers, confetti pieces, pictures from magazines, foam shapes, printed clip art, construction paper, artificial flowers, markers, and crayons. You can also have some "real" items available such as grass clippings, seeds, shells, etc. Think of other supplies to represent objects, such as cotton balls for clouds.
- Print copies of the Day 1 craft resource on printer paper. Cut out the individual rectangles, which contain the words of Genesis 1:1. Each child will need one rectangle. This resource can be found on our blog at http://smallpublishing.wordpress.com.
- Create a few sample collages. Each collage can reflect a different aspect of God's Creation. For example, one collage might show an underwater scene, one might display a rainforest environment, one might illustrate the night sky, and another collage might show a snowy landscape. Be creative!

- Shortly before the children arrive, pour some white glue on several trays or recycled plastic lids. Two or three children can share one tray of glue. The children will use paintbrushes to apply the glue to their collages.

Teaching Instructions:

- Today, we are making Creation Collages to show some things that God created.
- We have lots of supplies available for you to use on your Creation Collages, but please do not touch any of them yet.
- I have a few sample collages I want to show you. They show different parts of God's Creation.
- Raise your hand if you would like to name one thing you see on these collages that God created. *(Allow children to share their responses.)*
- These collages remind us of many things that God created. On each collage is our Bible memory verse from Genesis 1:1. *(Read the verse to the children.)* God is the One who created all these things.
- I am going to give each of you one of these plates (or trays) on which you will create your own Creation Collage. An adult is going to write your name on the back of the plate with a permanent marker.
- Once your name is written on your plate, you may turn it over and begin choosing some supplies to use for your collage. We will have to share with our friends so everyone has the opportunity to use the supplies.
- There are trays of glue to share as well. You will use a paintbrush to spread the glue on your collage.
- I am also going to give you a paper with the Bible memory verse on it. Choose a spot on the front of your collage to glue your memory verse.
- Be creative as you illustrate God's Creation on your collage!

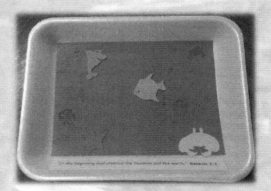

DAY 2: Craft
Recycled Birdfeeders

Supplies Needed:

- Clean, empty 59-64 oz. drink cartons
- Masking tape
- Colored pencils
- Twine
- Birdseed
- Small paper bags

Preparation:

- Collect empty drink cartons from your congregation and community. Rinse the cartons thoroughly, and allow them to dry.
- Cut out rectangular shapes from the middle of two opposite sides of each drink carton.
- Cover each carton with a few layers of masking tape, creating a plain canvas for the children to decorate.
- Design a sample craft to show the children.

Teaching Instructions:

- During our time at Camp Genesis, we have been talking about the truths that God created the entire world and cares for all He has made.
- The Bible tells us that God sees everything and knows every little creature. The Bible says God sees even the smallest sparrows. Sparrows are small birds. God is the One who gives them the food they eat.
- If God cares for the little sparrows, we know that God cares for us too. God wants us to trust that He cares for us. God knows exactly what we need. He knows all about us, and God loves us very much.
- We are going to make birdfeeders to remind us that God cares for the little birds, that God cares for all of His Creation, and that God cares for each of us.

- Listen first for instructions before touching the craft supplies.
- You will each receive one drink carton that looks like this. *(Hold up a covered, empty drink carton for the children to see.)*
- An adult will write your name on the bottom of your drink carton with a permanent marker.
- You can see that there are holes in two sides of the birdfeeder. This is so we can put the birdseed inside and the birds can get to it.
- We have covered each drink carton with masking tape, and now you get to decorate the outside and make it special. You can use the colored pencils to draw pictures and decorate your birdfeeder. You can also write words on it, such as "God cares for me."
- After you are finished decorating your birdfeeder, bring it to an adult leader, who will place a scoop of birdseed in it. The leader will also help you tape a length of twine to the top of the birdfeeder.
- Then, we will put your name on a paper bag and place your birdfeeder inside the bag, so you can take your birdfeeder home safely without losing any birdseed.
- The twine is on your birdfeeder so you can hang your birdfeeder outside in a tree in your yard when you get home. Then you can watch the birds that come and eat the bird food. When you see those birds, you can remember that God cares for those little birds. God cares for all of His Creation. He cares for each of us. God loves you very much.

DAY 3: Craft

Praise Rocks

Supplies Needed:

- Large, smooth rocks
- Acrylic paint
- Paintbrushes
- White glue
- Wiggle eyes
- Yarn
- Pom-poms
- Paper plates

Preparation:

- Create a sample craft to show the children.
- Cut some lengths of yarn for children to use as hair for their rocks, and cut several short pieces to be used as mouths.
- Place some white glue in trays or lids. Do the same with the paint. Have several paintbrushes available for children to use to apply the various colors of paint as well as the glue to their projects. Fill some cups of water for children to rinse their brushes in when switching colors of paint.

Teaching Instructions:

- The Bible tells us about a time when Jesus, God's Son, was riding into a city called Jerusalem. A crowd of people was shouting praises to God, but some other people who were there did not like it. They told Jesus to tell the people who were praising God to stop. But it was good for those people to praise God. Jesus said that if those people kept quiet and did not praise God, even the rocks and stones would cry out.
- Have you ever heard a rock talk? *(Allow children to respond.)* I have not.
- But, if this rock *did* start praising God, what do you think it might say? *(Allow children to respond.)*

- Today, you are each going to make your own Praise Rock to remind you that we should praise God, our Creator. God is good and He is worthy of our praise.
- Here is how we are going to decorate the rocks. Listen for instructions first before touching the supplies.
- You may paint your rock a solid color, or you can paint a patterned design on it. The paint is on trays for you to share with each other. Dip your paintbrush in a cup of water to rinse your brush off when you choose to use a different color of paint.
- There are also some supplies to glue on your rock to give it a face. There is some glue in front of you, and you can use a different paintbrush to put the glue on your rock. We do not want to use the same paintbrush for the paint and the glue, so there is more than one paintbrush for you to use.
- Choose two eyes and glue them on your rock.
- Glue some yarn on your rock to look like hair.
- Use a small piece of yarn to add a mouth to your rock.
- Choose one of the pom-poms to glue on your rock as a nose.
- When your rock is finished, we will write your name on a paper plate, and then put your rock on the plate to dry.

DAY 4: Craft

Plant People

Supplies Needed:

- Large foam cups
- Markers
- Potting soil
- Plastic spoons
- Grass seed
- Misting bottles with water
- Card stock
- Plastic drinking straws or craft sticks
- Small paper bags

Preparation:

- Make a few sample crafts ahead of time in order to give the grass seed time to grow so the children can see what their craft might look like after it has had time to grow.
- On card stock, print copies of the Day 4 craft resource, which contains the words "God makes me grow." Cut out and attach each rectangle to a plastic drinking straw or craft stick. Each child will need one. This will be inserted like a plant marker in the soil. This resource can be found on our blog at http://smallpublishing.wordpress.com.

Teaching Instructions:

- Boys and girls, I would like to introduce you to my plant person. *(Hold up a sample plant person for the children to see.)* We decorated the outside of this cup to look like a face, and the grass that is growing looks like hair!
- Today, you are each going to make a plant person. Each grass-haired cup person will be unique, just as God has made each one of us unique. We are all unique. We are one of a kind. We have different colors of eyes, hair, and skin. We like to do different things. Some of us are tall, and some of us are not as tall. But God is the One who makes us all grow. He helps us grow taller, learn new things, and become more like Jesus.

- Here is how you are going to make your plant people. Listen first for instructions and then I will tell you when you may begin using the supplies.
- We are going to give each of you a foam cup.
- When you have your cup, you can use the markers to draw a person's face on one side of the cup. Be careful not to press *too* hard, so it will not make any holes in your cup.
- Once the face is drawn, an adult will help you spoon some potting soil into the cup.
- Then we have some grass seed to put in our soil. The tall green grass starts as little seeds, but God makes the grass grow. An adult will help you sprinkle a layer of grass seed over the top of the soil, covering the entire surface.
- Then you will add a small layer of soil on top of the seed.
- Then we need to water our plants. Plants need water to help them grow. You will use a misting bottle to give your plant some water. We have to be careful not to overwater it, because *too* much water is not good for plants.
- Once you have watered your plant, we have a stick that says "God makes me grow" on it. You can place this stick down in your soil to remind you that just as God makes plants grow, He makes each of us grow too.
- When your plant person is all finished, we will put your name on the outside of a paper bag and place your cup carefully inside so you can take it home safely. You will have to be very careful when you carry it home, so the soil does not spill out of your cup.
- When you get home, take your cup out of the bag and put it in a safe place where it will not get knocked over. Be sure to find a place where your plant will get plenty of sunshine, because plants need sunlight to help them grow too.
- You will have to be patient as your plant grows; it will take some time. At first, you will not see anything growing. Then you might start to see some small blades of green grass peeking up through the soil. Then the grass should start getting taller.
- We can water our plants regularly and make sure they have enough sunlight. Then we wait as God makes them grow.

DAY 5: Craft
Stick Figure Families

Supplies Needed:

- Sticks/twigs
- Wiggle eyes
- White glue
- Green floral foam blocks
- Card stock
- Hot glue guns
- Paper plates

Preparation:

- Collect sticks and twigs of various shapes and sizes.
- On card stock, print copies of the Day 5 craft resource, which contains the words of today's Bible memory verse and the words "God made my family." Cut out the individual rectangles. Each child will need one. This printable resource can be found on our blog at http://smallpublishing.wordpress.com.
- Prepare a sample craft to represent your family.

Teaching Instructions:

- Today, we have a special project to remind us that God made our families.
- You are going to make your own stick figure family display. Here is my family. (*Hold up the sample craft, and tell the children a little about your family members. Point out which stick represents each individual in your family.*)
- Families are unique and come in all shapes and sizes. Each one is special, because God made our families. God made dads, moms, brothers, sisters, grandparents, uncles, aunts, and cousins. God made all of our family members.
- Here is what you will need to make your own stick figure family.
- Listen first to the instructions, and then I will tell you when it is time to pick up your supplies.

- You will each receive one foam block, which will be the base for your display.
- You will also receive a small rectangle that has today's Bible memory verse printed on it. (*Read the verse to the children.*) Glue this rectangle to the front of your foam block. (*Show the sample craft to the children.*)
- Choose one stick to represent each person in your family, including yourself.
- The sticks are different sizes, so you might choose a taller one for your dad and a little tiny one for your baby sister.
- Glue two wiggle eyes on each stick.
- Once all of your family members have eyes, decide in what order you would like your stick figure family members to be displayed.
- Push your stick figures down into the foam block so they are able to stand on their own. (Leave the figures where they are once you have pushed them into the foam so you will not create too many extra holes in the foam.)
- Then, raise your hand, and an adult leader will put some hot glue in each hole to help all of your sticks stand securely.
- When your stick figure family display is finished, we will write your name on a paper plate and put your project on the plate to dry.
- After the glue dries, you can take your project home and show your family. (It should be ready for you to take home after the carnival today.)
- Maybe you can find a special place in your house to put your stick figure family display so you will always remember that God made our families.

Special Note for the Leader:

- Children will have different numbers of twigs based on the size of their families. If the children's projects get too large with too many people included, encourage them to focus mainly on those in their immediate family, but be sensitive to the fact that many children may have several families and households of which they are a part.

Notes:

Camp Genesis:

Exploring God's Creation

Opening and Closing

Daily Leader's Guide

Small Publishing | Belleview, Florida

To the Opening and Closing Leader:

In Mark 10:14, Jesus said, "Let the little children come to me, and do not hinder them, for the kingdom of God belongs to such as these."

As a Camp Genesis volunteer, you're living out that very command. You have the great privilege and responsibility of helping children discover the truth of who God is and what He has done and of leading them to a faith-filled relationship with Him.

Please take a moment in prayer and ask God to prepare your heart as you seek to serve Him and His children. Remember, your job is to be a model of God's love.

When you're ready, turn the page and get ready to lead kids on an exciting adventure in God's Word as we discover His amazing Creation and get to know our great Creator!

*"The heavens declare the glory of God;
the skies proclaim the work of his hands."*
(Psalm 19:1)

Introduction for the Opening and Closing Leader

Daily Supplies Needed in the Opening and Closing:

- Computer
- Daily slideshow presentations
- Projector and projection screen
- Bible
- Music
- Offering containers
- Digital photos from daily activities

General Instructions for the Opening and Closing Leader:

- The daily opening and closing will be a time when all groups gather together to start and end their day at Camp Genesis. You will provide the first introduction to the day's theme as well as a final review at the end of each day. The opening and closing should be held in a large, central gathering place such as a sanctuary or auditorium.
- Slideshow presentations for each day's opening and closing are available on our blog. These contain slides of the rules, Bible memory verses, and other information. Advance the slides as you go through the outlines for each day's opening and closing.
- The following provides a general overview of each element of the opening and closing, highlighting the importance of each aspect and providing helpful suggestions. Specific outlines to follow for each day are found on the pages following this introduction.

General Overview of the Daily Opening:

- **Countdown**: A slideshow countdown timer is a helpful tool to assist you in getting started on time and gathering everyone. Begin the countdown a few minutes before the scheduled start time. The children will be working on an early arrival activity, but the countdown will be a signal and attention getter that the opening is about to begin. Children will understand that by the time the countdown is finished, they should be seated in their group's designated area for the opening. When the timer ends, you should have everyone's attention, and you can begin your opening greeting.

- **Welcome**: Speak with enthusiasm and enjoy your role as the opening leader. Your enthusiasm will be contagious and help to get the children excited about being at Camp Genesis. On the first day, you will want to give an overview of the entire program, giving them the name of the camp as well as your name and the church name and a brief explanation of the types of things they will learn and do throughout the program. Reassure them that they will have lots of fun, make new friends, and learn many new things about God and the Bible.
- **Schedule**: Describe the four activity stations to the children on the first day, so they will know what to expect during the rest of their time at Camp Genesis. Children will feel more secure with a consistent routine.
- **Rules**: Introduce the rules on the first day and review them each day. It is very important that the rules be reviewed each day, both for new children and for those who have been to Camp Genesis previously. Children need to know and be reminded of the boundaries and expectations. It is a good reminder for leaders as well, in order to help them be consistent with the children.
- **Offering**: Coordinate with the director of Camp Genesis to choose a missions project to support. Try to choose something that can be explained concretely to children, so they will understand how their offering is making a difference. Introduce the missions project to the children on the first day, and briefly remind them of the project each day. Encourage them to bring money, food, or other appropriate items throughout their time at camp to support this project. It would be helpful to send a note home to families to advise them that this will be collected. Each day during the opening, have the children bring their offering to the front during one of the songs. Have colorful containers in which they can place their offering. If you collect money, designate a trustworthy adult to put it away in a locked room after the opening, so it is not sitting out while the children are present.
- **Songs**: Select several songs to sing in each day's opening. Suggested songs can be found on the Small Publishing page on Pinterest. Add appropriate motions to the songs to help get the children involved and excited about singing. "The B-I-B-L-E" song should be sung each day as an introduction to the day's Bible memory verse.
- **Bible Memory Verse**: Each day, you will introduce a new Bible memory verse in the opening. With the words projected on the screen, read the verse slowly to the children. Briefly explain the meaning, paraphrase the verse, or explain any concepts that might be unfamiliar. Have the entire group of children and leaders read the verse with you. It is important to review the verse several times, since repetition will help it to stick in the children's minds. Each day, in addition to introducing the new verse, review those from previous days as well to help the children remember these.

- **Dismissal**: Ask the children to remain in their seats until you dismiss their group. Call the groups one at a time, and tell them what station they will be going to first. Remind them where the station is located, especially on the first day. Ask them to follow their group leader and walk quietly out of the sanctuary. Remind those who may be going outside or across a parking lot to be especially careful.

General Overview of the Daily Closing:

- **Welcome Back**: Greet the children as they arrive back in the sanctuary for the closing. As groups are arriving, have children raise their hands if they would like to share their favorite part of the day.
- **Photo Slideshow**: Have photographers take pictures of the children's activities throughout the day. If possible, have a slideshow of photos to play during the closing each day. Have a song playing in the background while the photos are projected on the screen. The children will enjoy seeing themselves and their friends on the screen. Try to have all children and groups represented in the slideshow, so no one feels left out.
- **Songs**: As you did for the opening, select several songs to sing in each day's closing as well. You may want to seek the children's input as to which songs to sing. As the week goes on and they become more familiar with the songs, they may tend to favor certain ones. Add appropriate motions to the songs to help get the children involved and excited about singing. Display the lyrics on the screen for the children if possible.
- **Bible Memory Verse**: Review the day's Bible memory verse. Have the children say the verse with you as it is projected on the screen. Since the children have been reviewing this verse throughout the various stations, challenge them to say the verse without looking at the words. Display a blank slide up on the screen and try to say the verse together as a group with no words showing. You can also review the Bible memory verses from previous days to help the children remember these.
- **Discussion Questions**: Children love being able to share their thoughts with the group. Having discussion and review questions relating to the day's topics and lessons will allow children to interact with you and each other and will also give leaders insight into whether the children are comprehending what they are learning. When you pose a question to the group, ask children to raise their hands if they would like to share their answers, wait several seconds to allow all children time to think, and then call on a few children to respond one at a time. Try to give some positive feedback to each child's response.
- **Prayer**: Encourage the children to close their eyes, bow their heads, and fold their hands for prayer time, so they are not distracted by what is going on around them. Explain to them that we are talking to God, and thus, we are to be very respectful. Lead the children in prayer, or ask another leader in advance if they would be willing to lead in prayer.

- **Reminders:** During these final moments, you may want to give the children a challenge relating to what they learned. Come up with a specific action they can go home and do that will apply what they learned that day. Encourage them to do it and then come back and tell you about it the next day. This closing time is also an opportunity to make any important announcements that pertain to the next day's activities. Reveal the next "color of the day" to the children. Remind the children to bring in an offering for the missions project. Encourage the children to bring a friend with them next time they come. You could also give them a hint about what they will be learning or doing the next day. Use this time to invite them to any special activities or church services you are having as well.
- **Dismissal:** Tell the children that they are to remain in their seats until they are dismissed. Distribute any fliers, crafts, or other items that need to be taken home. If your children's ministry does not already have a check-out procedure in place, you may want to consider implementing one for this program to make sure children are dismissed in a safe and efficient manner.

The outlines on the following pages detail the specific aspects to be covered during each day's opening and closing. It is best to keep a consistent routine as much as possible. However, there will be times when the outline will vary due to special activities for a specific day or due to time constraints. Watch the clock as you are leading, and adjust the schedule as necessary to fit the needs of your unique group. If you have extra time, add an additional song or review the Bible memory verses with the children again.

DAY 1: Opening

- *(When the countdown timer reaches zero, begin the opening by following the outline below.)*

Welcome:

- Welcome, campers! I want to welcome you to Camp Genesis. My name is _____, and I am so glad you are here at camp, because we have lots of fun things in store for you as we explore God's Creation together. God created this whole big world in which we live. He created me, and He created you. He created the sun, the moon, and the stars. He made the plants, the flowers, and the trees. He made all the animals too – the really big ones like lions and bears and elephants and the really small ones like birds and butterflies and goldfish. He made the oceans and all the creatures that live in them. As you can tell, there are lots of things in God's Creation to explore.
- I know that God created all of these things because He tells us about it in His special book called the Bible. (*Hold up a Bible for the children to see.*) The Bible tells us about how God created all of these things. At Camp Genesis, we are going to do some exploring in God's Word to help us learn more about God and all of the awesome things He made.

Song:

- We are going to sing a song together called "The B-I-B-L-E." That spells Bible. Let's stand and sing it together.
- (*Lead the children in singing "The B-I-B-L-E." Sing it through twice.*)

Bible Memory Verse:

- The Bible is a big book, but when we look in the very beginning of the Bible, it tells us about when God created the world. That makes sense to start at the beginning. In fact, the very first verse of the whole Bible is this: (*Show the Bible memory verse slide for Genesis 1:1 on the screen, and read it to the children.*)
- That is the verse. The bottom part is the reference. It tells us that the verse is in a book of the Bible called Genesis, which is what our camp (Camp Genesis) was named after. Those 1's mean it is in the *first* chapter of Genesis, and it is the *first* verse of that chapter. It is at the very beginning.
- I am going to read the verse again, and I want you to repeat after me.

- (*Divide the verse into small phrases. Say each part of the verse slowly, and have the children repeat the words after you.*)
- By the end of our time at Camp Genesis, we are going to try to know that verse by heart, so we will be able to say it without even looking at the words.
- This verse tells about what God created. He created the heavens, which are like the skies. He also created the earth, which is the planet on which we live. God made all these things.

Song:

- Let's sing another song to celebrate and praise our Creator.
- (*Lead the children in singing a song of your choice.*)

Schedule:

- As I said earlier, we have lots of fun things in store for you campers. Each time you come to Camp Genesis, we are going to start off together in this room for our opening. After our opening, we are going to split into four different groups. We have four different stations that you will go to throughout the night. At one station, you will have a snack. At one station, you will make a craft. At one station, you will participate in a fun game or activity. And at one station, you will do some exploring in the Bible and discover a special Bible truth.

Rules:

- I want to go over our camp rules with you. These will help us make sure everyone has a fun and safe time at Camp Genesis. (*Display the slide showing the four rules as you explain them.*)
- **Rule #1 – Walk, don't run.** We use our walking feet inside the church. We do not run when we are inside. We walk. If we are outside at games, and the leader says it is OK to run, then we can run, but we still have to be careful when we are crossing the street or the parking lot to make sure that we are with an adult and that we watch for cars driving by so we can be safe.
- **Rule #2 – Use inside voices.** When we are inside the church, we use our inside voices. We do not scream when we are inside. There will be other groups doing things in other rooms, and we do not want to bother or interrupt them, so we need to talk quietly. When we are outside and it is time for us to talk, then we can use louder outside voices, but when we are inside, we use our inside voices.
- **Rule #3 – Be respectful.** There are many different ways we can be respectful. This means that when a leader is talking, we listen respectfully. When it is a fellow camper's turn to talk, then we listen respectfully to that person, just as we want others to listen to us when we have something to say and it is our turn to talk.

- This rule also means we are respectful and do not hit, kick, or do anything that would hurt someone else. We do not bother other people, because we want to make sure they have a chance to listen. We use kind words that encourage and build up instead of putting people down, because there is no place at this camp for mean or hurtful words. At Camp Genesis, we treat each other with kindness and respect.
- We are also respectful of the church's property. We do not take things if they do not belong to us. We do not tear things up. We use our supplies carefully and respectfully.
- And when a leader asks us to do something, we obey them respectfully, because they are our leaders.
- **Rule #4 – Stay with your group.** This means you do not wander off from your group. You stay with your leaders and other campers in your group at all times. If you need to go to the bathroom, you need to ask your leader for permission first.
- All of your leaders know these rules and expect you to follow them. If there is a camper who has trouble following these rules, then that camper will have to miss some of the fun activities the rest of the group is doing. We have some fun things planned at camp, and I do not want any of you to have to miss them, so let's do our best to follow these rules. They are going to help us have a great time at camp!
- Do you have any questions about any of these rules? (*Allow children to respond.*) I want to make sure you understand them so you can follow them. If you do not have questions, I will assume you understand our rules, and I expect you to follow them.

Song:

- We are going to sing some more before we head to our first station.
- (*Lead the children in singing another song or two of your choice, as time allows.*)

Prayer:

- Before we head to our first station, let me pray with you, and then we will be on our way. When we pray, it means we are talking to God, so we want to be very respectful. We like to bow our heads, fold our hands, and close our eyes, so we are not distracted by other people or things around us. I will lead us as we talk to God. (*Lead the children in prayer.*)

Dismissal:

- Please stay in your seats until I dismiss your group.
- (*Call each group individually, and tell them which station they are going to first. Allow time for each group to exit before dismissing the next group.*)

  Group 1 – Creation Crafts   Group 2 – The Canteen Snacks
  Group 3 – Campfire Bible Stories   Group 4 – Adventure Trail Games

DAY 1: Closing

Welcome Back:

- Welcome back, campers! Who had a good first day at Camp Genesis? What was your favorite thing we did today? Raise your hand if you want to share.
- *(Call on several children to share their responses. Go ahead and start this discussion as the groups are arriving for the closing even if one group is running late.)*

Photo Slideshow:

- I hope you all had a great time exploring God's Creation – all the things God has made. Let's take a look back at all of the fun we had today. If you will look up at the screen, we have a fun picture slideshow for you!
- *(Play a slideshow of photos from the day. Have a song playing in the background.)*

Bible Memory Verse:

- Now, let's see if you remember our Bible memory verse.
- *(Show today's Bible memory verse slide on the screen. Read the verse with the children. Then, divide the verse into four parts, and assign each group one part of the verse. Have them say their parts in turn. Have everyone say the reference together. You can have them repeat the verse several times and challenge them to say it faster, say it in a whisper, say it without looking at the words, etc.)*
- I have a challenge for you to do at home. I want you to look in your Bible and see if you can find this verse in there. Remember, it is in Genesis at the very beginning of your Bible. Practice saying this verse and see if you can say it when you come back to Camp Genesis. Practice saying it to your brothers and sisters, your mom and dad, or your stuffed animals. Ask your parents to help you read through the Creation story again from your Bible, and tell them about all the things God created each day. Bring your Bibles back to Camp Genesis too, because we will have another awesome verse to explore together!

Song:

- Let's sing together.
- *(Lead the children in singing a song of your choice.)*

Reminders:

- *(Display the "Next Time at Camp Genesis" slide on the screen.)*
- A lot of us wore blue today, because it was the color of the day. During our next day of Camp Genesis, the color of the day will be red. Wear something red, and invite a friend to come with you.
- Also, during our time at Camp Genesis, we will be participating in a special missions project. *(Describe the specific project you have chosen to support.)* Ask your parents if you can bring an offering to Camp Genesis to help support this project.

Song:

- Let's sing another song before we leave.
- *(Lead the children in singing another song of your choice if time allows.)*

Prayer:

- Before we leave, let's pray together. After we pray, I want you to stay in your seats, and then I will tell you how we are going to dismiss you to go home.
- *(Lead the children in prayer, or ask your pastor or ministry leader to lead the group in prayer. This would be a good way to introduce that individual to the children.)*

Dismissal:

- Each day when it is time to go home, we are going to stay in this room until you are dismissed. *(Explain your specific dismissal procedures and rules to the children. For safety, it is important that children are not dismissed outside until a parent or guardian is present.)*
- *(Remind children to pick up their craft projects before leaving.)*
- *(You can lead the children in singing additional songs, reviewing the Bible memory verse, or talking more about the day's activities while you are waiting for parents to arrive.)*

DAY 2: Opening

- *(When the countdown timer reaches zero, begin the opening by following the outline below.)*

Welcome:

- Welcome back to Camp Genesis, where we are exploring God's Creation! I am glad to see some old friends and some new friends too!

Song:

- Let's start off a song. Stand with me, and let's sing together!
- *(Lead the children in singing a song of your choice, preferably one you sang on Day 1.)*

Discussion:

- Last time at Camp Genesis, we talked about many things that God created. Who can name one thing God made? Please raise your hand if you would like to share one. *(Call on several children to respond.)*

Bible Memory Verse Review:

- Do you remember the Bible memory verse we learned last time at Camp Genesis? It talked about how God made the heavens and the earth.
- *(Review Genesis 1:1 with the children. Show it on the screen, and have the children say it with you. Encourage them to say it without looking at the screen if they are able.)*

Song:

- Before we introduce today's Bible memory verse, we are going to sing "The B-I-B-L-E" together. *(Lead the children in singing "The B-I-B-L-E.")*

Bible Memory Verse:

- Today, we are talking about how God cares for all of His Creation. We have another memory verse from the Bible to learn today. This one is from 1 Peter 5:7.
- *(Show today's Bible memory verse on the screen, and read it to the children. Then, have them repeat it with you.)* This verse tells us that we can talk to God about our worries and fears, and we can trust that He cares about us.

Song:

- God cares about you very much. You are special to Him, and He loves you. Last time at Camp Genesis, we talked about many different creatures God made. God made humans special. He made each of us unique, and He loves and cares for us. Let's sing a song to thank God for creating us and caring for us.
- *(Lead the children in singing another song of your choice.)*

Rules:

- I want to go over our camp rules for all of our new friends who were not here before and as a reminder to all of us. *(Show the camp rules slide on the screen, and review them with the children.)*
    - Rule #1 – Walk, don't run.
    - Rule #2 – Use inside voices.
    - Rule #3 – Be respectful.
    - Rule #4 – Stay with your group.

Offering:

- As you know, we are working on a very special missions project during our time at Camp Genesis. *(Remind the children what missions project you have chosen to support.)*
- During our next song, if you have any offering you would like to give to our missions project, you can walk up to the front and put it in these offering containers during the song.
- *(Lead the children in singing a song of your choice. Allow children to bring their offering to the front during the song.)*

Prayer:

- Before we are dismissed to our stations, let's pray together. Please close your eyes, fold your hands, and bow your heads. *(Lead the children in prayer.)*

Dismissal:

- Please stay in your seats until I dismiss your group.
- *(Call each group individually, and tell them which station they are going to first. Allow time for each group to exit before dismissing the next group.)*
    - Group 1 – Creation Crafts
    - Group 2 – The Canteen Snacks
    - Group 3 – Campfire Bible Stories
    - Group 4 – Adventure Trail Games

DAY 2: Closing

Welcome Back:

- Welcome back, campers. What was your favorite part of the day at Camp Genesis? (*Ask children to raise their hands if they would like to share their responses. Go ahead and start this discussion as the groups are arriving for the closing even if one group is running late.*)

Photo Slideshow:

- We had a great day as we learned that God cares for His Creation. Let's look back at some fun moments from today.
- (*Play a slideshow of photos from the day. Have a song playing in the background.*)

Discussion:

- I am so thankful that God made me and that He cares for me and you and for all of His Creation! God cares for all of His Creation, and God wants us to care for His Creation too. Today, we are going to think of ways we can care for God's Creation.
- **How can we care for the earth God created?** (*Show the slide that corresponds with this discussion question.*) Raise your hand if you would like to share one way. (*Allow children to respond.*)
- *Examples: We can care for God's earth by recycling and making sure we do not litter (that means we throw our trash away in a trash can, not just on the ground). Our birdfeeder crafts were made from juice cartons. Instead of throwing these juice cartons away and creating more trash, we reused them to make something new. That helps keep God's earth clean.*
- God also created all of the animals on earth and instructed humans to rule over them. **How can we care for the animals God created?** (*Show the slide that corresponds with this discussion question. Allow children to respond.*)
- *Examples: We can take care of our pets. We can give them water. We do not want to hurt them. We can feed our fish. We can walk our dogs. We can clean our hamsters' cages. We can volunteer at the animal shelter.*
- God also wants us to care for other people, whom He created. **What are some ways we can care for other people?** (*Show the slide that corresponds with this discussion question. Allow children to respond.*)
- *Examples: We can use kind words and actions. We can obey our parents. We can show God's love to other people. We can help someone who is sad or hurting. We can pray for others. We can invite them to come with us to church. We can tell them about Jesus and His love.*

Song:

- God cares for us. Let's sing praise to our great and loving Creator!
- *(Lead the children in singing a song of your choice.)*

Bible Memory Verse:

- God is so great, and He cares about each of us and loves us so much. He loves us so much that He sent Jesus to us. We can trust Him.
- Do you remember today's Bible memory verse? *(Review 1 Peter 5:7 with the children.)*

Prayer:

- God cares about us. Big things and small things, God cares about all things, and we can pray and talk to Him about anything and everything. Before we leave today, I would like to pray with you.
- *(If time allows, ask children if they have any prayer requests to share.)* What are some things you would like to pray about? Raise your hand if you have a prayer request to share. We can pray about anything and everything – big or small! *(Allow children to respond.)*
- *(Lead the children in prayer.)*

Reminders:

- My challenge for you today is to go home and pray! You can pray before bed. You can pray before you eat lunch tomorrow. You can pray for or with your dad and mom or your brothers and sisters. You can pray anytime and anywhere.
- *(Display the "Next Time at Camp Genesis" slide on the screen.)* Next time at Camp Genesis, we are going to be talking about praising God our Creator. The next color of the day will be purple. Invite a friend to come with you, and do not forget to bring some offering for our missions project if you are able.

Song:

- *(Lead the children in singing a song of your choice if time allows.)*

Dismissal:

- *(Remind the children of your dismissal procedures.)*
- *(Also, remind children to pick up their craft projects before leaving.)*
- *(You can lead the children in singing additional songs, reviewing the Bible memory verse, or talking more about the day's activities while you are waiting for parents to arrive.)*

DAY 3: Opening

- *(When the countdown timer reaches zero, begin the opening by following the outline below.)*

Welcome:

- Welcome back to Camp Genesis! So far, we have been talking about all of the things God has created and about how much He cares for His Creation. God is truly our awesome Creator. He is so good and so great, and we just want to praise Him!

Song:

- We can praise God by singing our praise to Him, so let's sing together.
- *(Lead the children in singing a song of your choice.)*

Bible Memory Verse Review:

- Our first Bible memory verse was Genesis 1:1. *(Show the verse on the screen.)* Let's say it together. *(Recite the verse with the children.)*
- Our second Bible memory verse talked about how much God cares for all of His Creation. It was from 1 Peter 5:7. *(Show the verse on the screen.)* Let's say this one together. *(Recite the verse with the children.)*
- Today, we are talking about praising God, our Creator. He is the One who made us, and He deserves our praise.

Song:

- Before we reveal our Bible memory verse for today, let's sing "The B-I-B-L-E."
- *(Lead the children in singing "The B-I-B-L-E.")*

Bible Memory Verse:

- Here is our Bible memory verse for today. *(Show today's Bible memory verse on the screen.)* It is found in Psalm 150:6. *(Read the verse slowly to the children. Then, have them read it with you. Divide the verse, including the reference, into four parts. Assign each group a different part, and let the groups say their lines in turn.)*
- To "praise" God means that we celebrate how good He is. We tell how great God is! We tell about His great love and all His care. We praise Him because He is God. We praise Him for who He is and for the things He has done. God is so good, and we want to tell about how good He is and thank Him for all His works.

Song:

- We praise God because He made us. He is the One who created us. Let's sing our praise to God with this next song.
- *(Lead the children in singing a song of your choice to praise God.)*

Offering:

- We praise God because He is so great and loves us so much. He is God, our Creator.
- Let's praise God some more as we sing about how great He is. During this song, if you brought any offering for our missions project, you can bring it up front and place it in the offering containers.
- *(Lead the children in singing a song of your choice. Allow children to bring their offering to the front during the song.)*

Rules:

- I want to go over our camp rules for all of our new friends who were not here before and as a reminder to all of us. *(Show the camp rules slide on the screen, and review them with the children.)*
    - Rule #1 – Walk, don't run.
    - Rule #2 – Use inside voices.
    - Rule #3 – Be respectful.
    - Rule #4 – Stay with your group.

Prayer:

- Before we are dismissed to our stations, let's pray together. Please close your eyes, fold your hands, and bow your heads. *(Lead the children in prayer.)*

Dismissal:

- Please stay in your seats until I dismiss your group.
- *(Call each group individually, and tell them which station they are going to first. Allow time for each group to exit before dismissing the next group.)*
    - Group 1 – Creation Crafts
    - Group 2 – The Canteen Snacks
    - Group 3 – Campfire Bible Stories
    - Group 4 – Adventure Trail Games
- *(The game station may be held in a different location than normal today. If so, give the groups instructions as to where to go for this station.)*

DAY 3: Closing

Welcome Back:

- Welcome back, campers. What was your favorite part of the day at Camp Genesis? (*Ask children to raise their hands if they would like to share their responses. Go ahead and start this discussion as the groups are arriving for the closing even if one group is running late.*)

Photo Slideshow:

- We had a great day as we praised God, our Creator. Let's look back at some fun moments from today.
- (*Play a slideshow of photos from the day. Have a song playing in the background.*)

Song:

- God really is awesome, isn't He? We want to praise Him for how awesome He is. Let's sing His praise together.
- (*Lead the children in singing a song of your choice.*)

Bible Memory Verse:

- God created the heavens and the earth, and all of Creation teaches us about God and about how great He is.
- Do you remember today's Bible memory verse? (*Review Psalm 150:6 with the children. Challenge the children to say it without looking at the words if they can.*)

Discussion:

- We have been praising God a lot today, but we can never praise God enough! Since we have breath, then we should praise the Lord, just like our Bible memory verse says.
- (*Put the next slide up on the screen.*) Up on the screen, there is a sentence with a blank at the end. I want you to think about how you would fill in that blank. It says: "I want to praise God because _____."
- How would you finish this sentence? Raise your hand if you would like to share one reason you want to praise God. You can just say, "I want to praise God because," and then fill in the blank with your reason to praise God. I would love to hear from everyone, because there are so many reasons to praise God!
- (*Allow children to share their responses. Allow each child at least one turn if possible.*)

Song:

- There are so many reasons to praise God. Let's continue praising Him by singing together.
- *(Lead the children in another song if time permits.)*

Reminders:

- Next time at Camp Genesis, we are going to talk about how God makes us grow. Just as the grass grows and the trees and plants grow, God helps us grow too.
- *(Display the "Next Time at Camp Genesis" slide on the screen.)*
- I want you to wear the color green next time, because green will be our color of the day. Invite a friend to come with you, and remember to ask your parents if you can bring in an offering for our missions project.

Prayer:

- Before we leave, let's pray together. *(Lead the children in prayer.)*

Dismissal:

- *(Remind the children of your dismissal procedures.)*
- *(Also, remind children to pick up their craft projects before leaving. Today's crafts may still have wet paint, so it may be necessary to leave them to dry until the next day of camp.)*
- *(You can lead the children in singing additional songs, reviewing the Bible memory verse, or talking more about the day's activities while you are waiting for parents to arrive.)*

DAY 4: Opening

- *(When the countdown timer reaches zero, begin the opening by following the outline below.)*

Welcome and Bible Memory Verse Review:

- Welcome, campers! We have been having a wonderful time at Camp Genesis so far!
- We have learned that God created the heavens and the earth. *(Display the Genesis 1:1 memory verse slide, and read it with the children.)*
- We have learned that God cares for His Creation. *(Display the 1 Peter 5:7 memory verse slide, and read it with the children.)*
- We have learned that God, our Creator, deserves our praise. *(Display the Psalm 150:6 memory verse slide, and read it with the children.)*
- Today, we are learning that God is the One who makes us grow.

Song:

- Before we reveal today's Bible memory verse, let's sing "The B-I-B-L-E."
- *(Lead the children in singing "The B-I-B-L-E.")*

Bible Memory Verse:

- Today's Bible memory verse is found in Galatians 5:22-23. *(Show today's Bible memory verse on the screen. Read the verse slowly to the children. Then, read it again, a few words at a time, and have the children repeat after you.)*
- Today, we are talking about how God makes us grow. God is the One who makes the plants, the trees, and the grass grow. God is also the One who makes us grow. We grow taller and stronger, and we learn new things. God also wants to help us grow to be more like Jesus.
- God created all kinds of trees that have good fruit growing on them. God wants to help good things grow in our lives too. That is what this verse is talking about. The fruit of the Spirit is not fruit that you eat, but it is referring to the good things that grow in our lives when God's Spirit lives in us.
- Let's read this verse together again. *(Read the verse with the children.)*

Offering:

- As we sing our next song, if you brought any offering, you may bring it up front and place it in the offering containers.

- (*Lead the children in singing a song of your choice. Allow children to bring their offering to the front during the song.*)

Reminders:

- We only have one day of Camp Genesis left after today, so remember to bring in an offering next time if you are able. Also, on our last day of Camp Genesis, we are going to be having something very special, and that is a closing family night carnival! During the last part of our last day at Camp Genesis, we will have a carnival with games and activities, and your families are invited to join us for that. We have a note for you to take home to your parents and families to give them more information about it, but I wanted to let you know about it now. I think it is going to be lots of fun!

Rules:

- I want to go over our camp rules for all of our new friends who were not here before and as a reminder to all of us. (*Show the camp rules slide on the screen, and review them with the children.*)
    - Rule #1 – Walk, don't run.
    - Rule #2 – Use inside voices.
    - Rule #3 – Be respectful.
    - Rule #4 – Stay with your group.
- If any of our campers have trouble following these rules, they might have to miss out on some of our carnival time. I do not want you to have to miss out on the carnival, because I think it will be fun, so let's do our best to follow these rules.

Songs:

- Now, let's sing together!
- (*Lead the children in singing a couple of songs of your choice.*)

Prayer:

- Before we head to our first station, let's pray together. Please close your eyes, fold your hands, and bow your heads. (*Lead the children in prayer.*)

Dismissal:

- Please stay in your seats until I dismiss your group.
- (*Call each group individually, and tell them which station they are going to first. Allow time for each group to exit before dismissing the next group.*)
    - Group 1 – Creation Crafts
    - Group 2 – The Canteen Snacks
    - Group 3 – Campfire Bible Stories
    - Group 4 – Adventure Trail Games

DAY 4: Closing

Welcome Back:

- Welcome back, campers. What was your favorite part of the day at Camp Genesis? (*Ask children to raise their hands if they would like to share their responses. Go ahead and start this discussion as the groups are arriving for the closing even if one group is running late.*)

Photo Slideshow:

- We had a wonderful day as we learned that God makes us grow. Let's look back at some fun moments from today.
- (*Play a slideshow of photos from the day. Have a song playing in the background.*)

Bible Memory Verse:

- When we have God's Spirit living in us, He helps us grow to be more like Jesus. Then, we have good things growing in our lives – the fruit of the Spirit, just like today's Bible memory verse says.
- Do you remember today's Bible memory verse? (*Review Galatians 5:22-23 with the children. Encourage them to try to recite it with you without looking at the words.*)

Bible Memory Verse Review:

- Let's look back at our Bible memory verses from all week.
- (*Review Genesis 1:1, 1 Peter 5:7, and Psalm 150:6 with the children.*)

Songs:

- We can grow and learn more about Jesus when we read our Bibles and pray. This next song talks about how God can help us grow to be more like Jesus when we read our Bibles and pray every day. Let's stand up and sing this one together.
- (*Lead the children in singing "Read Your Bible, Pray Every Day."*)
- We want to keep learning from our Bibles and praying, so we can grow to be more like Jesus.
- (*Lead the children in singing another song of your choice.*)

Reminders:

- *(Display the "Next Time at Camp Genesis" slide on the screen.)*
- We only have one more day of Camp Genesis left, so remember to bring your offering for our missions project, and invite your family and friends to come with you for our special closing carnival.
- Remember, you will come at the normal time, and we will have our opening time and two stations. Then, your families can join us, and we will have our family night carnival with games and activities for you and your families to enjoy.
- We will be talking about the fact that God made our families, so invite your dads and moms, grandpas and grandmas, brothers and sisters, and cousins to come join us for the family night carnival. Tell your family to wear the color orange, because that will be our color of the day.

Prayer:

- Before we leave, let's pray together. *(Lead the children in prayer.)*

Song:

- *(If time allows, lead the children in singing another song of your choice.)*

Dismissal:

- *(Remind the children of your dismissal procedures.)*
- *(Also, remind children to pick up their craft projects before leaving.)*
- *(You can lead the children in singing additional songs, reviewing the Bible memory verse, or talking more about the day's activities while you are waiting for parents to arrive.)*

DAY 5: Opening

- *(When the countdown timer reaches zero, begin the opening by following the outline below.)*

Welcome:

- Today, we will learn that God made our families. We will celebrate by having our special family carnival later today! I know you are very excited for that!

Song:

- Our Bible memory verse for today talks about family, but before we reveal what our verse of the day is, let's sing "The B-I-B-L-E."
- *(Lead the children in singing "The B-I-B-L-E.")*

Bible Memory Verse:

- Today's Bible memory verse is Joshua 24:15. *(Show today's Bible memory verse on the screen. Read the verse slowly to the children. Then, have the children say it with you.)*
- God is the One who created all of our families. God wants our families to follow Him and love Him. God loves our families and knows what is best for us.

Song:

- Let's sing a song to celebrate the fact that God cares for our families. *(Lead the children in singing "He's Got the Whole World in His Hands." For each verse, substitute the words "the whole world" for the names of family members such as "our dads and our moms," "our grandpas and our grandmas," "our uncles and our aunts," and "our brothers and our sisters.")*

Bible Memory Verse Review:

- *(As you review each verse with the children, have the words displayed on the screen.)*
- God is the One who created our families. He created the heavens and the earth, just as our first memory verse, Genesis 1:1, said. Let's say it together. *(Say the verse with the children.)*
- God cares for our families. God cares for all of His Creation. Our second memory verse, 1 Peter 5:7, taught us that. Let's say that verse together. *(Say the verse with the children.)*

- We can praise God for giving us each a special and unique family. Our third memory verse, Psalm 150:6, talked about praising God. Let's say it together. (*Say the verse with the children.*)
- God wants to help our families grow more like Jesus. Our fourth Bible verse, Galatians 5:22-23, talked about that. Let's say it together. (*Say the verse with the children.*)
- Today's memory verse, Joshua 24:15, declares that we will choose to serve the Lord. I pray that you and all of your families will choose to love and follow God. I know that is my choice. Let's say today's Bible verse together. (*Say the verse with the children.*)

Song:

- (*Lead the children in singing a song. "I Have Decided to Follow Jesus" would be a good choice.*)

Offering:

- During our next song, if you brought any offering, you may bring it up front and place it in the offering containers. (*Lead the children in singing a song of your choice. Allow children to bring their offering to the front during the song.*)

Rules:

- I want to go over our camp rules as a reminder to all of us. (*Show the camp rules slide on the screen, and review them with the children.*)
    - Rule #1 – Walk, don't run.
    - Rule #2 – Use inside voices.
    - Rule #3 – Be respectful.
    - Rule #4 – Stay with your group.

Prayer:

- Before we head to our stations, let's pray together. (*Lead the children in prayer.*)

Dismissal:

- Because of the carnival, our stations will be a little different today. During our normal station time, you will only be going to Campfire Bible Stories and Creation Crafts. The snack and game stations will be included as part of the carnival.
- You will be joining one other group for crafts and the Bible lesson. That means there will be twice as many people as normal at each station, so I expect you to be extra good listeners for your leaders today.
- Group 1 and Group 2, you will both be going to Campfire Bible Stories first.
- (*Allow time for these groups to exit before dismissing the next two groups.*)
- Group 3 and Group 4, you will both be heading to the Creation Crafts station.

DAY 5: Closing

- *(Encourage parents and family members who have arrived for the family night carnival to sit with their children for this closing gathering.)*

Welcome Back:

- Welcome back, campers! I hope you have had a good day at Camp Genesis so far. Since this is our last day of camp, I would like you to think back over the five days we have spent together and tell me what your absolute favorite thing about camp was. Raise your hand if you want to share.
- *(Call on several children to share their responses. Go ahead and start this discussion as the groups are arriving for the closing, even if one group is running late.)*

Bible Memory Verse Review:

- During our time at Camp Genesis, we have made many new friends and discovered many new things about God our Creator and about this world He created.
- We learned five Bible memory verses during our time at camp. Let's say them together. We will put them up on the screen so your families can read them with us, but campers, see if you can say them without looking at the words.
- On the first day of camp, we learned that God created the heavens and the earth. Let's say Genesis 1:1 together. *(Display the Genesis 1:1 memory verse slide, and say it with the children.)*
- On the second day of camp, we learned that God cares for His Creation. Let's say 1 Peter 5:7 together. *(Display the 1 Peter 5:7 memory verse slide, and say it with the children.)*
- On the third day of camp, we learned that God, our Creator, deserves our praise. Let's say Psalm 150:6 together. *(Display the Psalm 150:6 memory verse slide, and say it with the children.)*
- On the fourth day of camp, we learned that God is the One who makes us grow. Let's say Galatians 5:22-23 together. *(Display the Galatians 5:22-23 memory verse slide, and say it with the children.)*
- Today, we are learning and celebrating the fact that God made our families. Let's say Joshua 24:15 together. *(Display the Joshua 24:15 memory verse slide, and say it with the children.)*

Photo Slideshow:

- We truly have had a wonderful time at Camp Genesis. Today, we have a photo slideshow with pictures from all five days of camp so our families can see what we have been doing and learning.
- (*Today's slideshow of pictures should include photos of activities from all five days of camp if possible. It can be a little longer than the usual daily slideshows to give parents and family members a glimpse at the activities from each day. Have a song playing in the background.*)

Thank You:

- We need to give our station leaders and group leaders a big "thank you" for all they have done to make our experience at Camp Genesis so much fun, so let's give them a big round of applause. (*Lead the children in clapping and telling their leaders "thank you."*)
- We also need to give a big "thank you" to our parents, grandparents, and friends who have brought us to camp each day and allowed us to come. Let's tell them "thank you" as well. (*Lead the children in clapping and telling their family members "thank you."*)

Certificate Presentation:

- I also want to tell each of you campers thank you for coming and joining us at Camp Genesis. It would not have been the same without you! We have a special certificate to give each of you for attending camp with us. When I call your name, please walk up front to receive your certificate.
- (*As you call each child's name, have your pastor or ministry leader hand the certificates to each child.*)

Reminders and Rules:

- Now it is almost time for our carnival! There are several carnival games and activities set up for you to enjoy. There is a snack station where you will decorate some snacks to look like your family members. There is also a family photo booth in one room, so make sure your family visits that station and has your picture taken together.
- During the carnival time, you do not have to stay with your regular group as you have during the rest of camp. You may go to the stations as you would like with your family or friends. But, please remember that our other rules still apply. (*Show the camp rules slide on the screen.*) We walk and do not run. This is very important since we may be going up and down stairs. We use our inside voices. We show respect to other people, to our leaders, and to the church property. We do not go in rooms that we do not belong in, and we do not bother things in the room that do not have to do with the game we are playing in that room. Let's follow the rules and have a great carnival.

- (*Give the children any specific rules you have for your carnival. Also, give the families directions as to where the carnival activities are located if they are spread out in various areas of the church or ministry facility.*)
- Before you leave at the end of the carnival, be sure to pick up the craft you made today. Also, when you leave to go home, there will be a leader at the door who will hand you a treat bag as your prize for participating in the carnival activities.
- (*Explain to the parents and families any special dismissal procedures. You may need to have a volunteer stationed at the registration table during the entire carnival so parents or guardians can sign their children out when they leave, since there will not be a formal closing gathering from which children are dismissed as usual and some families may choose to leave early. Be sure also to have adult volunteers near each door to serve as security guards to make sure no children leave during the carnival without a parent, guardian, or leader.*)
- (*Give families the details about any special weekend services you will be having and invite them to join you. You may also want to add a special invitation to these services in the treat bags.*)

Prayer:

- Before we begin our carnival, our pastor is going to lead us as we pray and talk to God. Let's close our eyes, bow our heads, and fold our hands. (*Ask your pastor or ministry leader to lead the group in prayer.*)

Dismissal:

- (*When dismissing the children to the carnival, you may want to dismiss only a few groups or rows of families at a time to help maintain order.*)

Notes:

Notes:

Daily Bible Memory Verses

NIV

Day 1: Genesis 1:1

"In the beginning God created the heavens and the earth."

Day 2: 1 Peter 5:7

"Cast all your anxiety on him because he cares for you."

Day 3: Psalm 150:6

"Let everything that has breath praise the Lord."

Day 4: Galatians 5:22-23

"But the fruit of the Spirit is love, joy, peace, forbearance, kindness, goodness, faithfulness, gentleness and self-control."

Day 5: Joshua 24:15

"But as for me and my household, we will serve the Lord."

In the beginning God created the heavens and the earth.

(Genesis 1:1)

But the fruit of the Spirit is love, joy, peace, forbearance, kindness, goodness, faithfulness, gentleness and self-control.

(Galatians 5:22-23)

Daily Bible Memory Verses

KJV

Day 1: Genesis 1:1

"In the beginning God created the heaven and the earth."

Day 2: 1 Peter 5:7

"Casting all your care upon him; for he careth for you."

Day 3: Psalm 150:6

"Let every thing that hath breath praise the Lord."

Day 4: Galatians 5:22-23

"But the fruit of the Spirit is love, joy, peace, longsuffering, gentleness, goodness, faith, meekness, temperance."

Day 5: Joshua 24:15

"But as for me and my house, we will serve the Lord."

In the beginning God created the heaven and the earth.

(Genesis 1:1 KJV)

But the fruit of the Spirit is love, joy, peace, longsuffering, gentleness, goodness, faith, meekness, temperance. (Galatians 5:22-23 KJV)

Notes:

Discover More on Social Media

Check out our Pinterest page and blog for decorating ideas, music suggestions, and more Camp Genesis inspiration.

When you use this curriculum in your ministry, please share your experiences with us!

- *What worked well?*
- *What would you do differently next time?*
- *How did you see God work through your program?*
- *How did the children respond?*

Comment on our Facebook page or send us an email.

Share ideas and photos to help inspire and encourage other ministries.

(Be sure you have parent permission before sharing photos of children.)

Small Publishing

P.O. Box 800, Belleview, FL 34421

smallpublishing1@gmail.com

smallpublishing.wordpress.com

facebook.com/SmallPublishing

pinterest.com/SmallPublishing

instagram.com/SmallPublishing

twitter.com/SmallPublishing

About Camp Genesis

Camp Genesis leads children on an exciting exploration of both God's Word and His Creation, building a foundation of faith in their lives as they get to know their Creator better. Through fun games, creative crafts, tasty snacks, and interactive Bible lessons, children will discover God's care for all of His Creation — each family, each child. As children take a closer look at God's created world, may their response be to praise the Creator who designed it all and put their trust in Him.

This curriculum contains five days of lessons, crafts, snacks, and games that can be used in a variety of ministry settings including Vacation Bible School, day camps, mid-week programs, or other events.

About the Author

Vanessa Small holds a bachelor's degree in children's ministry and biblical literature from Indiana Wesleyan University. She has been serving in children's ministry since she was in junior high school and currently serves as the children's director at her local church. She is also the author of several children's books and the *Ministry Gift Book* series from Small Publishing.

About Small Publishing

Small Publishing is dedicated to providing children, families, and churches with resources designed to educate, equip, and encourage faith development.

Notes:

Made in the USA
Columbia, SC
12 July 2019